Chapter 1

Hell slammed into town on a summer morning of overwhelming heat. While the poor knelt to pray and members of the nobility sipped their martinis, rocket fire and bomb blasts shook them all. Thus began the war on terrorism, a religious war pitting the powerful Christian West against the emerging Muslim countries of the East.

In December 1992, the United Nations undertook a military operation in the drought-stricken country of Somalia called Operation Restore Hope. Blue-helmeted UN peacekeepers and American Marines swarmed the countryside in an effort to bring peace to the war-torn country in Northeast Africa. Their job was to reopen roads controlled by militias to allow UN food shipments to be delivered to cities and villages. The Marines' large guns and no-nonsense approach to war brought a momentary order to the country, making it possible for blue-helmeted troops to provide policing support to the lawless country. Innocent Somalia people who had been starved for months by the warring militias received shipments of food, and the country finally possessed a measure of stability.

Unknown to the Marines and UN, terrorists had already infiltrated the country. Led and financed by Osama bin Laden—then a lesser-known leader—money, fighters and weapons landed in countries bordering Somalia. Muslim fundamentalist soldiers then infiltrated the countries' borders and moved into position outside the capitol city of Mogadishu. On June 5, 1993, Somalia militia and members of al-Qaeda ambushed twenty-four Pakistani soldiers, ultimately drawing American forces into a battle they could not win. This battle signaled a change in world politics and set the stage for the attack on the World Trade Center in New York.

The defeat in Somalia and attack on New York together signaled the beginning of the War on Terror. However, no conflict is an original conflict. That is to say, each conflict is a continuance of a war that came before it. This war is a continuation of the European Crusades (1095-1291), a war that changed the course of European and Middle Eastern civilization.

Like the War on Terror, the Crusades were a conflict of religion and a battle for money and power. The Crusades began when Pope Urban II stood before a crowd at a knight's tournament in France in 1095, declared the end of the world was near and issued a call to crusade. The people responded with fervor. The call to crusade tore down social and emotional boundaries that had prevented people from otherwise leaving their lords and the fields despite the stranglehold of feudalism. The people of Europe flocked back to the cities looking for work and hope, only to find themselves once again surrounded by starvation and suffering. However, gather they did, forming a group called the First Crusade that marched out of Cologne, Germany. The motley group of 40,000 knights, wives and camp followers marched east, gathering more people along the way. At each town, the horde would stop and ask, "Is this Jerusalem?" Eventually, the army peaked at 300,000, though attacks by locals defending their villages from the crusaders would downside the army to 100,000 people.

The First Crusade was defeated, but subsequent Crusades followed. Eventually the crusaders would take Jerusalem, and the transplanted Europeans would struggle to adapt to a new culture with new rules for survival. In this new environment, spies and assassins were everywhere and the threat of open rebellion by the Muslim population was always present. Tribal rivalries kept the Arabian people disorganized until Saladin of Tekrit, Iraq, organized a force of Arab Muslims and began to fight back. Under his command, the people of the Middle East reclaimed Jerusalem in 1187, and the European crusaders gradually retreated to Europe.

Fast forward to 1905: The discovery of oil again brought the Europeans back to the Middle East, this time bringing with them a new nation of transplanted peoples, the Americans. What resulted was a festering resentment fueled by changes in economics where the Americans and British were seen as power brokers. Their failure in policy is the world's failure.

Until the end of World War II, the oil-rich nations of Iran, Saudi Arabia and Iraq were agricultural or nomadic societies. However, beneath all that land were immense deposits of oil that would drive automobiles, industry and the power of nations. The British and Russians were the first to see the opportunity. They moved in and battled one another with political wit to control the oilfields of Iran. The British used the fear of communism to intimidate the people of southern Iran, while the Russians used the fear of British rule to force the northern people of Iran into cooperation.

When World War II began, Russia and Britain became allies to fight Germany's aggression. After the bombing of Pearl Harbor by the Japanese, the U.S. lend-lease law of 1941-1945 brought 30,000 American troops and millions of tons of equipment, such as tanks, airplanes and trucks, into Iran. In the meantime, a change in power in Russia forced the Russian military to quit its territory in Iran, leaving it to the British. The end of World War II left the British Empire seriously weakened. It gave up

Iran to the Americans and went home. The Americans were now the sole foreign power in the Middle East.

The Americans immediately went to work building a military infrastructure with the idea of creating a buffer between the aggressive, expansionist Soviet Union and the democratic West. The plan was to build an economy that would lift the people of Iran out of poverty. Instead, it tore the country apart. The CIA, by way of coup, established its own version of an Iranian government, installing a leader who turned its savage CIA-born intelligence organization, Sazman-e Etela' at Va Amniyat-e Keshvar (SAVAK), against its own people. The Iranian people, fearful of the secret police, rebelled against the CIA to oust the shah (king of kings). Only then did they realize they had been hijacked by Muslim fundamentalist Ayatollah Khomeini.

On the opposite side of the Persian Gulf in Saudi Arabia, the king was searching for a way to transition his country from an old world nomadic culture to a modern society. In the 1930s, King Ibn Saud of Saudi Arabia needed to raise money for his kingdom. He hired Karl Twitchell, an American from California, to search for gold and water. In his search, he discovered water, but no gold. Twitchell convinced the king he could attract more investment money if he stopped searching for gold and dug for oil.

The king agreed, and the Saudi Arabian/American oil partnership, the Aramco Company, was born. It sunk dry well after dry well until finally hitting oil in March 1938. The first well, Dammam Number 7, dug in Dhahran, produced 32 million barrels of oil until its closure in 1982.

The end of World War II brought the United States and Saudi Arabia into a closer relationship. In February 1945, forty-eight members of the House of Saud pitched tents and tethered sheep on the deck of the warship *USS Quincy* off the coast of Saudi Arabia. President Roosevelt and the king cemented a relationship that survived beyond the lives of the two leaders.

In 1943, a banner year for Saudi Arabia, four new wells—Abqaiq, Qatif, Ain Dar and Fadhili—were discovered. Saudis began construction of a pipeline to transport the oil from Dhahran to Lebanon. The logistics needed for the construction project were immense, but a San Francisco-based construction company, Bechtel Corp., proved up to the task. The project was a boon for the company that would, with no competitors, go on to build ports, airports, cities, factories and schools for the Kingdom.

Then Iraq entered the picture. In September 1980, Iraq, under the leadership of Saddam Hussein, launched an unsuccessful attack against its neighbor, Iran. Saddam's goal was to capture the Iranian oilfields and increase Iraqi dominance of the Middle East. After eight years of war, Iraq was partially occupied and unable to win. The United States government stepped in and provided intelligence and chemical agents to Iraq in an attempt to push out the menacing Iranian military. Saddam used chemical gas, first against the Iranian military and then against his Kurdish population in the north. The gassing of the Kurdish people was horrific, but the American government continued to supply weapons of mass destruction to Saddam.

During the Iran-Iraq War, the government of Kuwait saw an opportunity to seize the Rumailia oilfield beneath the Kuwait-Iraq border. With the go-ahead from the American government, Kuwait annexed 900 miles of Iraqi territory atop the oilfield. The Kuwaiti Army and oil businesses crossed the Iraq-Kuwaiti border and reestablished a new Kuwaiti border inside Iraq.

The Iran-Iraq War ended, and Saddam turned his attention to his southern border with Kuwait. He attempted to negotiate with the Kuwaiti and American governments, but the Americans refused. Saddam then invaded Kuwait to take back the Rumailia oilfield.

At this point, the American government sent soldiers to defend Saudi Arabia and began a public relations campaign run by the politically savvy public relations firm Hill & Knowlton. Almost immediately, and seemingly out of nowhere, appeared a pretty, articulate fifteen-year-old Kuwaiti girl rescued from

the clutches of Iraqi intelligence. She sat before the
Congressional Human Rights Caucus and spun her tales of
woe.

The public relations campaign went into overdrive designing
bumper stickers, T-shirts, and news articles funded by a group
called Citizens for a Free Kuwait. Americans across the nation
slapped the bumper stickers on their cars and wore "Free
Kuwait" T-shirts in support of a nation most Americans
previously never knew existed. The Pentagon worked overtime
to produce video footage and news stories of the invasion in
Kuwait. Overnight, the American public acted like
geographical/political media-trained experts on the oil-
producing country of Kuwait.

The Saudi Arabian government was immediately alarmed by
the invasion. Members of the royal family could not agree on
how to respond. Osama bin Laden offered 100,000 *mujahedin*
to attack Iraqi forces in Kuwait. Others wanted to pay off
Saddam. A third group wanted to settle the dispute through the
Arab League. The American government requested consent

from Saudi Arabia to station troops in the Kingdom of Saudi Arabia. After much discussion among the royal family, King Saud gave his permission.

American and coalition forces leaped into action. The United States Air Force began moving fighters and ground attack planes into the kingdom. The Army's airborne division suddenly had a new address in the Saudi desert. The Marine Corps sent a unit of infantry and infantry support from 3rd Marine Division on amphibious landing ships from Okinawa, Japan, and the Philippines. If Iraqi troops crossed the Kuwaiti border into Saudi Arabia, the Marines were to make a daring amphibious landing, cutting off supply lines. The unit had neither tanks nor air support, and, if ordered to carry out the mission, the troops were not expected to survive beyond a few days of hard combat.

The First Gulf War would not have been fought without the close alliance of the American and Saudi Arabian governments. This alliance was founded on oil and the economic interests of two of the world's most powerful families, the Saudi royal family and the Bush family. The relationship started with an airplane, oil and Texas. The Bushes, although from New England, fell in love with Texas for the same reason as the Saudis: oil. Both families flew planes. The Saud's bought planes and flew them for recreation. The Bushes flew them in defense of their country. Both families loved money and the power it brought. However, it would be oil and the airplane that would ultimately bring the two families into conflict.

King Fahd bin Abdul Aziz Al Saud (1921-2005), king and prime minister of Saudi Arabia, had many children. Some of them chose to live and adopt the Western culture. Others chose a path similar to that of bin Laden and shunned the West and became ultra-fundamentalist Muslims. In his youth, bin Laden attended college in Lebanon and was known for drinking champagne and driving a loud, yellow sports car. His pilgrimage to Mecca (Hajj) changed his life and the course of history. After his pilgrimage, he dropped his adolescent ways and adopted a strict Muslim lifestyle.

Across the ocean in the New World, a former WWII fighter pilot named George Herbert Walker Bush Sr. had children of his own. One of those children, George Walker Bush Jr., would grow up to emulate his father. George W. became a fighter pilot like his father, attended the same university, worked in the oil fields of Texas, ran for election, became president in 2001 and later attacked the same country as his father had.

The Saudi kingdom built strong family ties with the wealthy and influential Bush family, but it also did business with another well-liked and respected America president, Ronald Reagan. In 1982, President Reagan had wanted to supply weapons to an anti-communist rebel army in Nicaragua. When Congress and the House of Representatives refused to fund arms to the Contras, Reagan turned to the House of Saud for help. The Saudis wanted anti-air missiles, and Reagan wanted money for arms. The American administration secretly flew 400 missiles to Saudi Arabia and, in return, received $32 million to fund the war against the leftist government of

Nicaragua. The American-Saudi relationship survived and prospered for many years.

Then on Sept. 11, 2001, members of bin Laden's al-Qaeda group hijacked four planes carrying passengers. Terrorist pilots on two of those planes, American Airlines Flight 11 and United Airlines Flight 175 from Boston, targeted and destroyed the World Trade Center Towers. A third, American Airlines Flight 77 from Washington-Dulles International Airport, crashed into the Pentagon. Passengers of the fourth plane, United Airlines Flight 93 flying out of Newark, N.J., attempted to regain control of the plane. In response, the hijackers crashed the plane into a field outside Pittsburgh, Pa.

America retaliated by invading Afghanistan and destroying the ruling Taliban government. In 2003, American and British forces invaded Iraq and overthrew Saddam. Today, America fights the war against terrorism on many fronts. The destruction of the twin towers was devastating for New York and the country. Terrorist cells in San Francisco were active in planning and training for what could have been their next big attack.

The American West Coast has been seemingly unaffected by the terrorist attacks on the East Coast. There is reason to believe al-Qaeda chose the West Coast as a training ground to carry out attacks on the East. One of the first terrorist cells found in the United States was discovered in Santa Clara, Calif., just one hour south of San Francisco. Technology is what attracts terrorists to the southern part of the Bay Area, specifically Silicon Valley. Many, if not most, of the foreign-born terrorists have studied engineering, and, as they have demonstrated in the media, they are adept with Internet technology. The importance of technology is one of the very few things the East and West can agree upon.

For example, shortly after the invasion of Afghanistan by U.S. forces and just before the invasion of Iraq, protesters from all over the world took to the streets of San Francisco en masse. For over a week, downtown San Francisco's financial district was in chaos as protesters staged marches and sit-ins.

Protesters used computers and cell phones to communicate times and locations. Lookouts standing on street corners sent text messages to small groups and individuals who would suddenly congregate in a location to block traffic and shout slogans. As police moved into position, the group split back into small groups or individuals and disappeared to re-form into new locations.

The atmosphere of downtown San Francisco was serious yet festive. Early into the protests, police were tipped off to bottles of gas and rags hidden along protest routes. The protesters themselves came from different parts of the world and various social and economic backgrounds. The participants ranged from high school students to adults. A small minority were veteran protesters of the 1960s, now with kids, watching their newly minted "radical sons and daughters" hauled away by police just as they had been during the Vietnam War. Most of the new protesters, however, would not have fit the description of the '60s hippie.

Standing in the shadows of the protesters were the terrorists who had arrived in Silicon Valley before 9/11. Even after the protests lost steam and protesters left for home, the terrorists remained in the area, watching, waiting and training.

Chapter 2

On Oct. 3, 1993, in the far-flung capitol city of Mogadishu, Somalia, the forces of the West and the East collided in pitched battle. After two days of combat, seventeen American Army Rangers died and sixty-nine were wounded. The opposing forces led by Osama bin Laden suffered 500 to 1,500 casualties. Compared with other historical battles, the number of casualties on both sides proved minuscule, and the so-called winning side lost the highest number of combatants. It signaled a new face of warfare and change in world politics.

Before the Battle of Mogadishu, armies of the Middle East had confronted armies of the West in conventional warfare, using tanks, artillery and large formations of troops. After the Gulf Wars, the armies of the Middle East learned that the tanks of the Western armies were too powerful. So they began to conduct unconventional warfare, meaning small groups of shadow units dressed as civilians attacking lightly defended civilian targets.

In 1993, the Horn of Africa may have seemed like a long-forgotten place, but it is and has been of vital importance. Somalia, at the tip of the horn, is a country smaller than Texas, dwarfed by the omnipotence of the United States, Great Britain, France, Russia and China. The United Nations' Operation Restore Hope was not intended as a sacrifice for Somali national sovereignty or precious resources, but rather for social stability. The on-again, off-again conflict, which began in 1977, had wrecked the country. The UN operation launched a military operation to deliver food and hope to a country whose young people could only remember war and starvation. To the American public, it was a gesture of good will. For the military, it was a clear mission with a structured objective and an exit plan. Americans did not want a conflict that would preempt the country into a long, drawn-out war.

The nine bloody years in Vietnam with its endless casualties and failed diplomacy still haunted America. The struggle in

Somalia was intended as a struggle for peace and prosperity, not material gain. "Mission creep," the political buzzword of the day, was deeply feared by the American public because of other projects that had expanded beyond their original goals. But it happened anyway, not because of American policy, but because of a request from the UN. The UN wanted to apprehend Somali warlord Gen. Muhammed Farah Aideed to bring stability to the country. Up to this point, Aideed (of the Habr Gidr sub-clan) and Ali Mahdi Mohamed (of the Abgal sub-clan) had been fighting an ongoing civil war for control of the country. Many Somalis starved because warlords had used them as political ammunition to fight each other.

The UN had two military organizations supporting its operations in Somalia. The blue-helmeted peacekeeping troops were not equipped for sustained combat. They were present only to provide stability and support to the local population. The second, the United States Marine Corps, carried out small-unit warfare tactics against an elusive enemy attacking from back alleys. Unlike the blue-helmeted United Nations police force, the Marines landed with equipment needed to conduct offensive operations. Their fighter aircraft controlled the skies, helicopters pinned down fighters and tanks crushed enemy positions. With the Marines present, the warlords could not stay in one place for very long. The militias learned their lesson early in the campaign and kept quiet, waiting for the Marines to leave.

By October 1993, the Marines were gone, leaving behind the lightly armed Army Rangers and a unit of the U.S. Army 10th Mountain Division under Pakistani command. This leveled the tactical playing field. Now the lightly armed Rangers had to defend themselves against a city full of Somali militiamen with machine guns, sniper rifles and rocket-propelled grenade anti-tank weapons. The Marines had been the law of the land, and the law had left town.

In addition, the Somali warlords had allies. The Islamic fundamentalists of Tehran viewed the peacekeepers as an American-led invasion force occupying the Horn of Africa. Tehran and the terrorist organization al-Qaeda (the Base) had decided the Americans presented a threat to the spread of fundamentalist Islam in Africa. Al-Qaeda could not conventionally oppose the Western powers with military force; however, it could limit its influence with small-unit terrorist action.

For al-Qaeda, carrying out an operation like this would require a leader with the experience to conduct far-reaching operations. Bin Laden had the experience and money to coordinate the entire operation himself. Using profits from the bin Laden construction company and from donations, he flew militia fighters and weapons from their bases in the Middle East to neighboring Somalia countries. From these bases, the fighters infiltrated the country, taking up positions outside the capital city.

On Dec. 9, 1992, United States Marines and a Navy SEAL team, acting on orders of the UN, came ashore to secure the Mogadishu airport. Military Special Forces landed on the beach, searching for mines and beach obstacles, but instead found the spotlights of media cameras. The sight of SEALS on the beach in the dead of night with spotlights on them caused great disgust among the military, giving military personnel more reason to mistrust the media. The Pentagon had invited the broadcast media to observe the landing but neglected to cancel the invitation when the situation changed.

Between December 1992 and May 1993, Somalia experienced, for the first time, a relative period of calm. The Unified Task Force (UNITAF) was hit by small hit-and-run attacks, harassing in nature, but nothing that could dislodge UN forces or stop food distribution. However, after the June 5, 1993, ambush of twenty-four Pakistani soldiers, Gen. Muhammed Farah Aideed, an Italian- and Soviet-trained officer, could finally hope to return to his former rule of power-by-civil-war. The ambush of Pakistani forces in the city of Mogadishu destabilized the area, signaling a return to offensive operations by Aideed. The first snatch-raid intended to capture Aideed was carried out unsuccessfully in June by the Marines. The second attempt by Task Force Ranger in October is now called the Black Hawk Down incident.

Bin Laden wanted to push the Americans off the African Horn but needed Aideed's militia to make the attacks. Aideed needed bin Laden's money and logistical expertise to support his forces. To drive the Americans out, Aideed and bin Laden had to convince the American public that the situation was not worth the fight. His purpose was to bring the Americans into a climactic battle and cause significant casualties. All Aideed needed to do was wait for the Marines to leave. Without them, the Rangers would be surrounded by enemies in a dangerous country.

The ambush of the Pakistani soldiers in Somalia was not just another street battle. Al-Qaeda knew, or at least thought, that the United Nations would have to take some kind of action after the death of the soldiers. Outraged by the ambush, the UN passed Resolution 837, authorizing the use of force to capture Aideed. Per resolution, the U.S. Army put together Task Force Ranger, a mixed special-forces group of Rangers and Delta Force operators to seize Aideed. On Oct. 3, 1993, Task Force Ranger conducted a helicopter-borne assault into an area of the city called the "Black Sea." This area was deep inside the slums of Mogadishu where Aideed's headquarters were located.

Initially, the operation went as planned. Helicopters inserted Delta Force operators, who apprehended the prisoners without incident. When the supporting Rangers were inserted into Black Sea to cover the withdrawal of Delta Force, militiamen with rocket-propelled grenades (RPG) shot down two Black Hawk helicopters. Operations immediately began to rescue the pilots. With two helicopters down and convoys unable to reach them, all available friendly forces were cornered and pinned, so the Rangers lost the fight. A small light-infantry force requires speed and maneuverability to win. With their momentum lost, the Rangers quickly ran out of resources.

Gen. William Garrison, Task Force Ranger commander, requested assistance from the UN peacekeeping force unit commander, led by a Pakistani general. However, the relief operation did not begin for hours. To Americans, Operation Restore Hope was their chance to help people in a part of the world where even heaven had given up. Television screens across the world replayed scenes of Black Hawk helicopter pilot CW2 Michael Durant held in captivity and American bodies lying mutilated in the streets

The background for this scenario was that terrorist camps stretching from Sudan to Yemen and Somalia were already in place. In the mid-1980s, Tehran had organized a military group called Al-Quds forces, whose purpose was to expand radical fundamentalist Islam influence into the heart of Africa. Its strategy was to destabilize governments and then introduce Islam as a stabilizing change of choice. Thus, the terrorist camps.

When the United States Marines landed in Somalia in 1993, bin Laden had used his own financing to fly forces from Yemen into countries surrounding Somalia. Knowing he could not defeat the Marines, bin Laden waited until they left before confronting UN forces. The explosive series of attacks made after their departure came as no surprise to Marines patrolling the city who had already heard that message. In Kismayu, locals presented a petition and a live goat, requesting the Marine unit to stay. Nevertheless, the Marines loaded their tanks and helicopters and returned to the United States as scheduled.

They weren't completely gone. After the main force of 24,000 Marines left the country, smaller rotating amphibious unit(s) called a Marine Expeditionary Unit (MEU) remained aboard ships. Marines monitoring the situation discovered an increasing number of women leaving Mogadishu and a greater number of men moving in. The Islamic forces, when they attacked, were made up of citizens from Saudi Arabia, Iraqi intelligence, Lebanon, Somalia, Ethiopia and Eritrea.

How did Saddam Hussein get involved with al- Qaeda? It is somewhat unclear since, prior to 9/11, the U.S. was less focused on keeping track of terrorist groups. Groups changed names, and members changed groups frequently, keeping the situation fluid. However, it appears that when Saddam heard of Tehran's plans to attack the Americans in Somalia, he sent his son Uday to Tehran, asking that Iraqi intelligence lead the attack. Tehran never conceded control but did allow agents to be present.

Once Ranger forces were pinned down, Gen. Garrison went to the UN forces commander requesting assistance. Forces from Malaysia, Pakistan and the U.S. 10th Mountain Division were stationed at a football stadium, a short distance from the Black Sea area. However, it took many hours to organize the 100 vehicles and their personnel, and the forces were unable to respond to the situation for three hours, leaving the Rangers in the kill zone.

During the presidency of pro-Islamic leader President Benazir Bhutto, Pakistan made great efforts to appear pro-democratic to the West, but it had, in fact, colluded with its enemies. Once American forces left the Horn of Africa, Pakistan strengthened its alliance with North Korea and Tehran. Roads were built into Afghanistan to supply weapons to bin Laden. Pakistan used its position to fund and transport drugs for distribution to the West. Was the Pakistani commander coordinating his troops with those of bin Laden during the rescue effort of the

Rangers? We don't know. Organizing a vehicle-rescue operation takes time, and the Pakistanis had few vehicles of its own.

Pakistan may have set the ambush on its own troops. Third World countries tend to view the use of their troops differently than developed countries. Typical Third World countries poor in resources cannot manufacture rifles, helmets or trucks. People, however, are much more expendable. The rifle a soldier carries has a greater value than the soldier who carries it. For Pakistan, twenty-four soldiers are easily replaceable.

Persuading the American public to give up the Horn of Africa was not difficult because of the American public's view of Somalia. In this operation, Americans thought of their soldiers as rescuers, not as combatants. Nations do not send rescuers on rescue missions to die. The battle for Mogadishu was a victory for Tehran and bin Laden, and its outcome may have served as an impetus to launch an attack on the World Trade Center towers. The investment that bin Laden made in the ambush of the Rangers at Mogadishu paid enormous dividends for al-

Qaeda.

Chapter 3

To understand the roots of this modern-day religious war, one needs to travel back to 1095 A.D. when Pope Urban II stood in front of a crowd in Claremont, France. The occasion was a sporting event for knights, who traveled near and far to joust against one another for a purse of gold. Thousands of people assembled, and, at the tournament's end, the pope walked on stage and declared the end of the world was near. In just a few words, he denounced jousting and warfare between European fiefdoms and changed the future of Europe.

He told them the time had come to stop killing fellow Europeans and to take up arms against infidel Muslims. Killing infidels would absolve a Christian of all sins, and it was better to die killing nonbelievers than to die with sin. The pope's speech spread like wildfire from village to village. Knights kneeled, crosses painted on white linen worn over their armor.

They took an oath dedicating themselves to the Crusades. From Claremont, the pope journeyed from town to town giving the same awe-inspiring speech that would attracted a mass emigration of God-inspired warriors. The message to crusade came at a time when people all across Europe faced life alone in lands of highway robbery and lurking criminals. Large cities like London were filled with abandoned homes and factories. People felt alone, scared, hungry and subject to the indifference of feudal lords. At an individual level, the Crusades seemed like an answer to one's prayers. People's sins would be absolved, and loneliness would be lifted from their souls. At a political level, the sounds of war smelled like money. A call-to-arms meant a shift in population, loosening the powerful grip of the feudal lords on the sharecroppers. Before the Crusades, most people never left the vassal state. They seldom traveled to town, relying on the lord for news, education and work.

A noble's second son had no chance of inheritance because laws gave inheritance to the first son. The second and third sons traditionally went off to war to seek their fortunes. The feudal lords believed the Crusades to be an opportunity to gather more land and power, while the knights fought to succeed in life and therefore win a wife.

Making war on Muslims may not have seemed difficult to vassals. They knew little of the world outside their homes or feudal states. The Muslims spoke a different language and were a people who refused baptism. They hadn't been baptized, so they could not go to heaven, which, by church standards, was blasphemous.

The First Crusade was the most famous but least successful. It began in Cologne, gathering more followers as it marched on Constantinople. This first army was no disciplined army, merely a rabble of peasants and knights strung out for miles who didn't know where they were going. They followed an eccentric monk, Peter the Hermit, who led the way in an easterly direction. Peter was an odd figure; who rode a mule from town to town wearing a sack-like garment. In fact, he looked like a bearded sack seated on a mule. By modern standards, he would have been an alarming sight. But Peter covered hundreds of miles on that mule and attracted thousands of villagers to the cause of the Crusades.

Upon arrival at each town, someone went forward to ask a local if this was Jerusalem. Town by town, the mass of 300,000 people moved forward, taking liberties that under normal circumstances would have been criminal.

The route of the crusading mass could be followed by the trail of death it left behind. Jewish towns were particularly vulnerable. The crusaders slaughtered the inhabitants of Jewish villages before continuing onward. At Cologne, the mayor took pity on the fate of the Jews and opened the city gates so they could seek refuge inside. This incensed the crusaders who stormed the city walls and killed 10,000 Jews.

As the motley crew of followers traveled forward, its ranks grew larger, making leadership problematic. Eventually the group split into three. One group was led by Peter the Hermit, the second by a knight known as Walter the Penniless and the third by a monk named Gottchalk. Splitting into three groups made logistics much easier, but the walking crusaders depended on the good graces of the farmers and towns for food and water. Communication became a problem. When smaller groups of people became lost, they quit the Crusade and returned home.

When the crusaders entered Hungary, they found an abundance of food and water. The country was much poorer than France and Germany and homes were mere hovels and large towns did not exist, but they had food. Racked with starvation, the crusaders fell upon the Hungarian people like crazed dogs. Crusaders pillaged and burned food storages. No woman was safe from rape and kidnapping. At first, the Hungarians acted confused, unsure of the intentions of the invaders. The leaders called for order, imploring their followers to behave like Christians and control themselves. But soldiers and followers ignored the order and, instead, raped, pillaged and burned their way across Hungary.

The Hungarians became emboldened, determined to defend themselves. When crusaders came upon the town of Moysson, they expected to storm it and kill the people inside; instead, they walked into a trap. The villagers drove the crusaders from the town into the water of a raging river. Most crusaders slipped under the water's current and drowned. Those who survived crossed the river and didn't stop until they reached France. Once in France, their tale of woe quickly spread, making them the joke of Europe. Jokes, songs and stories of their flight from the poor villagers of Moysson traveled from mouth to mouth and country to country.

After the attack on the village, the Hungarians turned from being the hunted to the hunter. They lay in wait behind rocks, bushes, ponds, homes and trees. The mighty force of 300,000 that finally entered Constantinople was reduced to just 100,000 crusaders. The once-adventurous group of mayhem-makers appeared more like a starved mass, stumbling into town on their last slice of bread. The mayor welcomed them warmly and made room for their recovery on the outskirts of town. With a bit of rest, and food in their bellies, their spirits bounced back with vengeance. The knights wanted to cross the

Bosporus Straight into Muslim lands and take the fight to the enemy. However, the mayor resisted, saying they were in no condition to fight. The crusaders turned on the town, ransacking it until the mayor relented, just to get rid of them.

The crusaders crossed the Bosporus Straits into Nicomedia. Once landed, the leadership became quarrelsome and split. Peter the Hermit remained with his group in Nicomedia, while Walter the Penniless and Gottchalk set off in different directions. From this quarrel, a new and different group was formed that was led by Rainald.

Rainald successfully attacked the castle of Exorogorgon, but the victory was short-lived. That evening the knights held a merry feast, passed out and awoke the next morning to find themselves surrounded by the Muslim army. After eight days of searing heat, they could hold out no longer. With their water flasks dry and the city well outside the castle walls, they surrendered. Rainald and a small group of men who surrendered were allowed to live as soldiers of the Muslim army. The Muslims divided the rest into two groups. They first group was sold into slavery, and the second became human archery targets for Turkish bowmen practicing to perfect their aim.

Back in Nicomedia, Peter the Hermit had lost control of the crusaders who were pillaging the city. He gave up hope and crossed the straits on his own, returning to Constantinople. In the meantime, Walter the Penniless took action to avoid losing control of his group. He attacked the city of Civitot and, after a short fierce battle, lost his life and those of his followers, thus ended the First Crusade.

Or did it? As Peter the Hermit was leaving Cologne with his group of 300,000, another had begun to form. The second group was slow to organize and did not leave until later. In May 1097, the second group of 600,000 knights, archers and camp followers, traveling in four groups, arrived in Constantinople. Leading this second group were four men: Count Raymond of Toulouse, Godfrey de Bouillon and his brothers, the Count of Boulogne and the Duke of Lorraine. After crossing the Bosporus, they marched through a jungle to reach the city of Nicaea. There, they set mines in the walls of the city and, in one large explosion, ripped them open. Thinking the city defenseless, the crusaders bedded down for the night. The next morning, however, they awoke to find the wall repaired. It would take several more weeks for the Turks to finally give up and surrender the city.

This second group of 600,000 marched from Nicaea to Antioch, a crown jewel for the crusaders. If they were to prove themselves world conquerors, they would have to take Antioch. Their arrival, however, was not a surprise to the Turks. Spies had trailed the army since Constantinople. By the time the crusaders arrived, the defenders of Antioch were well-prepared. Seeing this, the Christians settled in for a long siege outside the city wall.

The Turks were not beginners to siege warfare. They kept the crusaders off- balance by sneaking outside the wall at night, attacking and then retreating inside. In the early morning hours, the Turks would once again exit the city to bury their dead.

Afterward, the Christians would dig up the bodies, decapitate them, and launch the heads over the wall.

After seven months of siege, Bohemond of Otranto made a secret deal with Firuz, one of the city's emirs. The deal was for Bohemond to become prince of the city when it was taken. In the meantime, word reached the Christian camp that Emir Kerboga of Mosul was approaching with 200,000 soldiers and eager for a fight. The word of his approach sent a shockwave through the Christian army. Its leaders worried that even the smallest of bad news might send many of the crusaders running for Constantinople. Then, suddenly, the siege was broken. Firuz opened the gates to the outer wall, and Bohemond and his crusaders stormed inside.

Outside the wall, Kerboga arrived with his reinforcements, only to find the city in Christian hands. Muslim forces engaged the Christians on a bridge entering the city. This bridge, when in Muslim hands, proved insurmountable to the attacking Christians. Now, the situation was reversed. Christians controlled the bridge, and the Muslim force of 200,000 was cut down by the dozens. Eventually, the Turks pulled back from the bridge but not out of the fight.

In Europe, news of the battle reached the kings who sent a fleet of ships to rescue the besieged crusaders. When they arrived, Kerboga captured and burned the ships. With all hopes of rescue gone, desperation filled the city. The Christian solders were nearly out of water, and they had eaten the horses and donkeys that had carried them from Europe. Yet, if they surrendered, they would become slaves or archery targets.

Enter into history a humble monk named Peter Bartholomew. Inside Antioch, Peter stood before the crowd of sick and dying crusaders and proclaimed that he'd had a vision from Christ. God came to him in the dead of night and commanded him to spread the word that Christian men must give up intercourse with Muslim women. Peter said he had seen the lance that pierced the side of Christ. Peter dug a lance from the ground and held it high in the air for all to see. The soldiers were so taken with the story that they spent three days fasting, giving alms, praying and confessing their sins. On the morning of the fourth day, the Papal Ligate held the lance in his hand, and the Crusaders marched outside the gate like zombies, arrows raining upon them from all directions. The crusaders, after days of fasting and praying, were in state of unstoppable psychological frenzy. Turkish soldiers became quickly unnerved at the sight of the Christian soldiers shot full of arrows and still advancing. What should have been a clear victory for the Turks turned into a complete rout of their army.

Peter had taken what seemed like a sure defeat and turned it into a momentous victory. When the battle was over, the victorious soldiers turned their attention to the lance. They felt victorious, but also duped. The Crusade was not as promised. They wanted proof that the lance was the one used to pierce the side of Christ. Unfortunately for Peter, the Papal Ligate died in battle, so the crusaders turned on Peter. To force him to prove his vision, the Normans built two huge fires reaching many yards in length and then forced Peter to walk across the ashes. When he emerged from the other side, the people were not satisfied. They forced him to walk the ashes a second time.

When he emerged unharmed once again, the people decided he was truly a spiritual being. They pushed their way forward and tore his hair and clothing. Peter suffered fatal injuries, but it is uncertain whether he died of burns or injuries from zealous crusaders.

For five months, the crusaders rested in Antioch; then they marched on Jerusalem. On June 7, 1099, Godfrey de Bouillon attacked Jerusalem, assaulting it from all sides. The initial attack had great momentum but failed. Only the outer wall was taken, leaving the inner wall intact and the city still in Turkish hands. Low on food, de Bouillon decided to lay siege and wait for supplies. The Turks were one step ahead of de Bouillon. They captured the supply caravans before they could reach the crusaders. Conditions for the Christians got so bad that men resorted to scooping foul water from the bottom of the supply vessels to satisfy their thirst.

On Thursday, June 13, the attack started once again, this time with two large siege towers pushed up to the city wall. Inside the city, the Turks (a.k.a. Saracens), in a taunt to the Christians, erected a cross calling it the "real Cross of Christ." Once again, overpowered by the desire of food and water and crazed by heat, the crusaders surged forward to attack. Raymond had convinced the city's emir that if he opened the gates, a bloodbath would be prevented. The emir, fearing for the lives of the people, opened the gates. The crusaders rushed forward, quickly forgetting their promise, and slaughtered the citizens of the city. With Jerusalem taken, the crusaders set aside their weapons and rested. And thus the First Crusade finally ended.

Tired of war, the soldiers settled into their new life of business and politics. As time passed, the transplanted Europeans found that the old customs from the cold climates of Europe did not work in the arid environment of Jerusalem. They tried to force the Muslims to convert to Christianity, to learn the European language and way of life. The princes, barons and other nobility intended to recreate their European lives in the desert. However, things did not work exactly as planned. The idea of feudalism fell apart. Sons were dying young, leaving the family without an heir. Why men died faster than women is not completely understood. One theory is that European men, in a quarrel, went for the sword rather than talking things out. In this new land of sand and heat, assassins were everywhere. A person had to be on guard at all times because he did not know who might be lurking about. Any innocent bystander could be a potential killer sent by a rival.

The new environment forced the newcomers to give up their outdated ideas, but in doing so, they gained much more in return. The Muslims were idealists. They understood mathematics, astronomy, physics and art. They already had knowledge of new medicines and medical techniques. Food and architecture were favorite pastimes for the desert people. They wanted beautiful cities and delicious food. All this was a big change for the Europeans who boiled meat and lived in large dark, dank castles. For them, medicine was cutting into a person's skull to relieve headaches. A library was a short stack of books pilled in the corner. The preparation of food was probably the best-learned skill for the crusaders. In Europe, people hoarded food because the supply was short and people starved to death in the winter months. Foods like fruits and bread were plentiful in the Middle East. So the Christians ate better and became healthier.

Of the new arrivals, the smarter tended to last the longest. The longer they stayed, the more they thrived. They learned the language of the Muslim people and adapted to the surroundings. In time, they became just as "Middle-Eastern" as the Middle-Easterners themselves.

In December 1145, the Muslim leader Zenghi sacked the city of Edessa, Greece. This enraged King Louis VII of France, who decided it was time to teach the nonbelievers a lesson. The recruitment drive for the Second Crusade went much like the first. Saint Bernard became its grand representative much like Peter the Hermit in the First Crusade. He went from town to town, speaking out for the cause. Again, droves of people flocked to the ranks. Their first order of business was to take back the city of Edessa from the Muslims.

However, just like before, the Christian army became entangled in other matters. Before reaching Edessa, the army attacked the Jews, followed by the Greeks, Moors and then the pagan Wendish people. The people fought back, and, by the time the second crusading army made it to Edessa, it was much smaller. King Louis decided he lacked the resources to attack Edessa and, instead, turned his attention to Damascus. When he arrived, he set up camp to rest. Zenghi was no fool and immediately attacked the tired Christian army. After four days of constant attack, the Christian crusaders lost heart and turned for home.

Although the quest to take Edessa failed, the Christians didn't have to face the fearsome leader Zenghi. Instead, Zenghi's own servant killed him. Zenghi had caught the servant taking wine and threatened to have him killed. Out of fear of his own life, the servant stabbed Zenghi in the heart. The failed Christian crusaders trotted back to Europe without incident.

During the occupation of the Middle East, the Europeans were able to control the land and laws but not its people. There was always an underlining threat of uprising. Attacks and assassinations were everyday occurrences. The Europeans were never comfortable with their governing role; consequently, they remained nervous about what each new day might bring. Muslims could carry out assassinations, but tribal differences prevented them from organizing forces to challenge the Christians. Until Saladin.

Saladin was born in Tekrit, Iraq, but raised in the customs of Damascus. He was a warrior, thinker, leader and man of vision. His vision was to rid Muslim territory of Christian invaders. In 1174, he launched a series of attacks, retaking city after city until his defeat at Telljezer by Baldwin IV. Though defeated in battle, he was allowed to slip away. In 1180, after many years of fighting, Saladin offered the Christians a truce, but they refused.

Reynald de Chatillon wanted to attack at the heart of resistance. He used camels to transport a fleet of ships over the desert floor to attack Medina and Mecca. The Muslims defeated Chatillon and his land-locked navy. Before attacking the cities, however, Reynald had captured and molested Saladin's sister, who was traveling in an unarmed caravan. This ruined any chances the Christians had of making a truce. Saladin chased the force of Reynald de Chatillon retreating across the desert to Hattim, west of Tiberius. In the ensuing battle, the Christian forces were defeated and Reynald captured. Reynald was then brought before Saladin who unceremoniously lopped off his head with a sword.

Then, on Sept. 17, Jerusalem, once crown jewel of the Christian Crusade, was surrounded. In a two-day battle, the Muslims retook the city. This caused uproar in Europe. To the Europeans, Jerusalem was theirs by right and must be retaken. The Church immediately declared that Christianity was at stake.

France's King Philip Augustus, Germany's Emperor Fredrick Barbarossa and England's King Richard the Lionheart declared themselves leaders of the Third Crusade. Fredrick, with his force of 100,000 men, crossed the Hellespont (Dardanelles) and recaptured Iconium; however, the advancement of the

German forces came to a halt when Fredrick died from swimming after dinner. His body was preserved in vinegar so it could be buried in Germany. However, the deceased king never made it back to his home country. The vinegar treatment failed, and his body deteriorated in the desert heat.

The remainder of the force took refuge in Antioch. Most of Fredrick's remains were buried here. His son tried to save the remaining bones for burial in Jerusalem. In the meantime, King Richard and King Philip and their troops had surrounded Acre. However, Muslims forces inside the city were receiving regular reinforcements, which forced the Christian forces to wait. Then, Saladin, his body racked with sickness, ordered his forces to retreat.

The battle of Acre was remembered more for the acts of Richard than the defeat of Saladin. Richard had a reputation as a romantic with a cruel streak. His love for women and his acts of intolerable cruelty are legendary. During the battle of Acre, Richard ordered the death of 2,700 Muslim prisoners when their arranged ransom failed to reach him in a timely manner.

During the Crusades, just like today, prisoners taken in war could return home if a ransom was paid. If the country refused, then it was up to the family. If the ransom remained unpaid, prisoners were either killed or enslaved. From then on, when young Saracen children refused to obey their parents, they were told that King Richard would come to take them away.

The battle for Acre was the climax for the Third Crusade. This time both sides had had enough and were ready for a treaty. On Sept. 2, 1192, Muslims forces and Christian crusaders signed a treaty giving Christian worshipper's access to Jerusalem. In February 1193, six months after the signing of the treaty, Saladin passed into a coma and died. Friends and foes mourned his passing. The Christians, it was said, admired his prowess and would have welcomed him to fight on their side any time.

Chapter 4

In 1212, twelve-year-old Stephen of Cloyes went to King Philip of France with what he claimed was a letter from Christ ordering him to organize a crusade to Jerusalem. Philip's first reaction was to send the boy back to his parents. Pope Innocent, however, saw this as an opportunity and gave his blessing, saying, "The very children put us to shame."

Thus began the Children's Crusades, a mass of 30,000 children with just a few adults walking from Vendome to Marseilles, France. That summer had been particularly tough on crops, making water and food scarce for the weary travelers. Many children either died or abandoned the crusade and returned home.

The remaining brood, after marching from town to town in the deadly summer heat, arrived at the port of Marseilles. Here, Stephen had promised that the sea would dry so they could cross to Jerusalem. However, the sea did not dry, and two scheming men, William the Pig and Hugh the Iron, promised to transport them on ships to Palestine, free of charge. The children agreed and climbed aboard seven ships. Along the way, the ships hit a storm and two of them sank on the island of San Pietro. The remaining five ships sailed to Bouige, Algeria. Once ashore, the children were divided into groups of five and sold into slavery. Egyptian Governor Sultan al-Kamil purchased 700 of them to use as interpreters and secretaries. Of the children who made it as far as Baghdad, eighteen were decapitated for refusing to submit to Islam. Nearly all the French children from the first Children's Crusade either died or disappeared. Of the 30,000 children, only one returned to France after eighteen years of slavery.

The first Children's Crusade encouraged a second copycat Children's Crusade. The second began with a boy named Nicholas, who persuaded approximately 20,000 German children to follow him through the Alps. The route was treacherous and, undoubtedly, some died, but others soldiered on until they reached Genoa, Italy. Once in Genoa, the governor turned away the rabble of starved youths, saying he would not have such a diseased bunch in his city. Some of them went to Rome, pleading to be excused from their pledge to crusade until they were older. Only 2,000 of the second Children's Crusade would survive to see home.

The Crusades were the invention of a religious group still active today. This elite group, the Knights of St. John, was made up of European men who swore to uphold the laws of Catholicism. Their obedience was not to kings but to the Vatican itself. Later they would be called The Knights of the Templar and still again renamed The Knights of Malta.

This group would be written into history as a powerful fighting force, rich in banking and real estate. However, their beginning came from a much more humble idea. The Knights of St. John organized under the idea of serving the poor and diseased. Their service began in Amalfi, Italy, where they cared for injured travelers coming back from the Crusade, and others on their way to Jerusalem. They provided food, shelter and medical treatment to the needy. Each knight took a monk's vow of poverty and chastity. The more sick and wounded they treated, the more educated they became in Middle Eastern culture. They learned Muslim politics and war tactics, which turned their idealism into military action.

A splinter group of the Knights of St. John took up the sword and swore to defend Christianity with their minds and bodies, and thus was born the Knights of the Templar. The Church blessed the organization, which became the pope's de facto military army. Their understanding of the Middle East and its politics made them the most powerful entity in the Crusades. Those wishing to sacrifice themselves for the cause went to the Templar for direction. In return for the Templar's cooperation, wealthy European nations contributed large donations to the organization. The remaining members of the Knights of St. John became the Knights Hospitaller, still caring for the sick and needy.

Each member of the Knights Templar wore a red cross on his tunic and, like their brothers, the Knights of St. John, swore themselves to chastity, poverty and the pope. Their leader was St. John the Evangelist, who sought recruits from far and wide. Selection was very exclusive, and only members of the nobility class could hold the rank of knight. When a new recruit entered the Templar, he was placed into one of three social classes. If he came from nobility, then he became a knight and wore the Red Cross. Those born of the middle class could be accepted, but not as knights. Each wore a tunic with a black cross and was given the rank of sergeant. Their task was not only to fight but also to serve as butler to the knight. The lowest, or third class, recruits made up administrative personnel.

While the knights swore themselves to poverty, the organization itself grew enormously rich from banking and donations. These donations came in forms of estates, membership and contributions from kings and princes, who hoped to call upon their services if needed. The group graciously accepted gifts from the nobility, but made no promises in return. The Templar received a lot in wealth, but gave just as much in blood. Moreover, they brought security to an unstable area.

The Knights of the Templar did much of this by acting as financiers. Loans with high interest rates were made so businesses could be opened and civil projects could be built. Local rulers built infrastructure projects that provided jobs to workers who invested in the local economy. The Templar's had their own set of laws, which made them neutral to state politics. Rulers could call on them to broker alliances and solve differences; however, these services did not come cheap, and, at times, the Templar gave their services to the highest bidder. They were even known to switch sides in battle. The Knights of the Templar owned castles and estates all across Europe. Kings became jealous and fearful. They gave money and sought favors, but behind doors schemed to bring the power of the Templar's to an end.

In the meantime, power had shifted in Egypt. In a 1260 rags-to-riches story, Baibars, a Muslim slave, climbed the military hierarchy until he reached the rank of general. He then assassinated Qutuz, the sultan of Egypt. Two years later, he marched with his army out of his castled cities and attacked the Christians.

This was the beginning of the end for the crusaders and the Templar's. From Nazareth, Baibars took castle after castle until marching on Acre, the final stronghold of the Templar's. For those still alive after years of crusading it would be their final bastion. The few Templar's who managed to survive the attack either blended in with the populace or climbed aboard ships and sailed to Malta. The fall of Acre put fear into the European nobility, which began fortifying the island of Malta, which bore the next order of knights, the Knights of Malta.

Back in Europe, the kings and princes smelled blood. King Philip of France had been secretly collecting information about the members of the Templar. In 1307, after years of rumor and politicizing against the religious group, he ordered the arrest of all knights. Most of those arrested went to trial and were then burned at the stake. Those who survived once again did so by scattering and blending in with the locals.

Today, the Templar still exists, but not at the level it once did. Officially, it is nonexistent, but unofficially, the organization is still active. Membership is still very selective, but now includes women. Those who are accepted do so by recommendation of another member. The knight's class is still made up members of the social elite, and sergeants are still recruited from the middle class. After the purge of King Philip, the Templar and surviving Hospitallers survived by providing medical and relief services on battlefields and in areas of disaster and poverty. The Knights of Malta still exists in Malta and in other countries. In the United States, AmeriCares provides Hospitaller with domestic and international relief, coordinating its relief efforts with the Order of Malta, Mother Teresa's Missionaries of Charity and others. Politically, the Knights of Malta are neutral and still act as a diplomatic go-between for governments. Members of the order have their own stamps, money and passports. They build hospitals and provide relief to devastated areas of the world. There are three groups of the Knights of Malta in the United States: the Federal Association in Washington, D.C.; the American Association in New York;

and the Western Association in California. As of 1999, there were 3,100 American members and 11,000 non-American members worldwide.

To say the Crusades were a vehicle for social change is an understatement. People were motivated at a personal level to make extraordinary sacrifices that have shaped the politics even of this century. The Children's Crusades, though perhaps misguided, made an enormous statement, demonstrating that the actions of young adults are often the impetus of policy. Groups like the Knights of St. John and the Knights of the Templar attracted like-minded individuals under a united cause, moving events in ways governments could not achieve. They did it much more rapidly and efficiently, which put them at odds with national policy.

Chapter 5

Stabilities the same, power to blame. Its idols we seek to turn us to lamé.

Anonymous

The clash of religion has always been difficult and bloody. But during these times of great social stress, the world moves forward into a period of significant change. We are masters of our destinies and we do have options. Choosing a path can be difficult. Not all paths are bad and not all are good.

The Sept. 11 attack on the World Trade Center towers set into motion a worldwide change. Economic and social ideals that worked before are becoming obsolete. We try to hold onto some of the old ideas because they are familiar and the future feels uncertain. However, in time we will discard them, acknowledging they have lost their usefulness.

Some governments of the Middle East, like Saudi Arabia, are making fundamental changes that will better serve the people.

Prior to 9/11 the Saudi Arabian government found itself moving ever closer to the political far right in order to meet fundamentalist demands. Its policy was to trade money for allegiance and, in so doing, paid off the fundamentalists who otherwise would have made attacks on Saudi Arabia itself.

Now, opposition to the government is committed to armed confrontation. Terrorist attacks inside their own countries have forced a shift in power. The government has been granting greater rights to the citizens, especially women, though this has been eroding in recent years. Cultural exposure to the West, particularly during the first Gulf War, made a schism between the leadership and the people. This led to problems between the Muslims and the Americans. The relationship that Saudi Arabia and America once enjoyed became strained, but survived and continues to build strength.

Americans are also undergoing social change. We are learning that we now have to share the power we once took for granted. The access of natural resources such as rare earth minerals can potentially be priced out of reach of America industry, shrinking the country's manufacturing output. As the level of manufacturing shrinks, so does the purchasing power of families who desire to send their children to universities. Because of this, fewer adults attend higher education, and the pool of qualified American workers shrinks further. The rising price of college tuition, the price of housing and the loss of pensions have made the military a greater attraction for young adults and their parents. Congress may increase benefits to soldiers, and citizens may see the military as a regular part of their life rather than just another option. All this makes for a smarter and better military. Also, the age limit to enter the Army is now forty, so older people are entering the military, which means greater maturity and life knowledge. The days of barracks conversation leading in with, "Man, I was with this girl Saturday night; what a freak" may be replaced with, "The controls in my La-Z-Boy went out; ya'll know what that's like." Troop field exercises will sound less like, "Let's take this fucking hill!" and more like, "Let's wait 'till the temperature drops." In other words, this is a trade-off because older people are slower and take fewer risks. Risk-taking on the battlefield is important because it can pay off with large dividends. Some soldiers who take risks in the moment of battle may die, but some won't. Call it luck or whatever, but bold maneuvering on a battlefield can turn the tide in an important battle.

Other changes in the offing are a move of political and economic power from the East Coast to the West Coast of the U.S and a rise of religion. Though declining in membership and influence in recent years, religion will take on a greater influence. Surrounding all this change are Christianity, Islam and Judaism.

Of the holy books associated with three vying religions, the Torah (400 BCE) is the oldest. The Bible and the Koran are ideas born of the Torah. However, of the three, the Koran (written 570-632 BCE) is one of the most influential in today's world. To understand the Muslim fundamentalist, a person must understand the words of the Koran. Its author, the Prophet Muhammad, lived in a world of violence, disease and slavery. He is not God, but a messenger who received the word of God. He is said to have traveled great distances, and it was from these travels that he learned a healthy respect for his fellow humans. Unlike other men of his time, he married someone older than himself and had a great respect toward women. He disliked slavery, but did not speak against it. He was a father, a husband and a lover of ideas.

People of vision and understanding wrote the religious text of Islam, Christianity and Judaism. These were writers subjected to the same real world problems and needs of the average person of their time. Because of this, the authors injected their personalities into the texts, and all personalities have imperfections and insecurities. This is the price of being human. Muhammad wrote the Koran during times of great social disenchantment, much like today. In knowing this, we can assume that the life and times of the Prophet Muhammad were violent.

To Muhammad, death was just another part of life and not something people should fear. War is a part of society, and the goal of the Muslim is to die in battle. The Koran divides people into two distinct groups. There are the "believers" (Muslims), who make up the majority, and the "non-believers" (everyone else). Some Jews and Christians can be "believers" but generally are not considered capable; Jews even less so. Nearly all Jews, Christians and the rest of the people of the world are "non-believers." "Believers" enjoy special privileges that the "non-believers" do not. These privileges extend only to men and not to women, who are of a lower class. All "non-believers" are destined for hell.

The No. 1enemy is the Jew. The Christian takes a distant second place. Most Christians are forgivable if they portray themselves properly toward God. With very few exceptions, Jews cannot make it into the world of the "believer." As you can see, Islam loathes Jews, believing that the Jews turned their back on God after he set them free from the tyranny of Egypt. Because America has chosen the side of the Jewish state, it is the largest enemy facing the Islamic fundamentalists.

"Believers, Jews, Christians and Sabaeans—whoever believes in God

and the Last Days and does what is right—shall be rewarded

by their lord.

Believers, take neither the Jew nor the Christians for your

friends. They are

friends with one another."

(Koran)

Muslims have used the Koran to legitimize their attacks on Christians and Jews. What the fundamentalists want is power. Consequently, the Koran has become the cookbook for action, used by both Muslims and Christians.

In March 2004, pictures of Iraqi prisoners from Abu Ghraib prison flashed hundreds of times across television screens and media airwaves. The pictures of prisoners stacked upon each other on the floor seemed odd. In response to the photos, media correspondents interviewed regular Iraqi people who said they were shocked and disgusted by such treatment of their fellow citizens. Insurgents who had captured an American, an antenna technician named Nick Berg, beheaded him in retaliation to the photos. The government launched an immediate and full investigation into the conduct of American soldiers guarding the prison.

All this seemed surreal, not because American soldiers treated prisoners badly, but because of the techniques themselves. Torturing of prisoners has happened in every war in the past and will continue as long as there is conflict. Younger soldiers tend to be more aggressive. They feel frustrated at taking enemy fire, angry that their friends are dying and helpless in stopping their deaths. Torture methods used by angry or revengeful soldiers, however, are much different from what was shown in the pictures. Typically, soldiers will burn prisoners with cigarettes, cut them with knives, starve them of desire for water and food or break bones. Not much personal gratification is gained by stacking naked people or forcing them to stand on a box with a blindfold, so there had to be other reasons behind this type of torture.

The soldiers whose personal lives were revealed by the media and government felt they had done what was right by following orders, something hammered into them at basic school or boot camp and training. Instead, the government prosecuted the enlisted soldiers and stripped the unit officers of their command.

Up to this point, the administration of Iraq had not been going smoothly. In fact, the American government very much underestimated the politics involved, hoping that by throwing money at the situation, it would resolve itself. However, as we all have learned, Middle Eastern politics is much more complicated. Pressuring the prisoners to talk was necessary to find the insurgents and stop the bombings, kidnappings and assassinations, which ultimately ceased reconstruction.

It was not from soldier's imagination that these techniques were used. Instead, passages were used from the Koran, methods which could be used to gain prisoners' cooperation. One of the first pictures to flash across the news screen was that of naked Iraqi prisoners stacked in a pile. This technique was taken from a verse of the Koran:

"God will separate the wicked from the just. He will heap all wicked one upon another and then cast them into Hell".

(The Spoils 8:37).

The second most-viewed photograph showed a person standing on a box with a hood covering his head and body with wires attached to his testicles.

"Garments of fire have been prepared for the unbelievers. Scalding hot water shall be poured upon their heads, melting their skins and that which is their bellies. They shall be lashed with rods of iron."

(Pilgrimage 22:19)

In response, the insurgents answered back with a passage of their choosing: "Give courage to the believers. I shall cast terror into the hearts of the infidels. Strike off their heads, strike off the very tips of their fingers!"

(The Spoils 8:12)

Using these techniques presents a problem for military commanders. The role of boot camp is to instill teamwork and discipline. Giving an order and then prosecuting a soldier for carrying it out undermines discipline. Imagine if a soldier could choose to either attack an enemy position or not. Could a commander charge a soldier with failing to carry out orders if the soldier felt that attacking the position was immoral? After this, maybe not. Such actions put the system of discipline in a quandary, a fact the government failed to think through.

Chapter 6

And the Egyptians shall know that I am the Lord, when I
stretch out My hand over Egypt and bring out the Israelites
from their midst. This Moses and Aaron did;
as the Lord commanded them, so they did.

Torah Exodus 7:5(JPS Hebrew-English Tanakh)

In the middle of the conflict between the East and the West is a
small country of Jewish faith. The presence of this faith angers
many of the Middle East who would prefer that the East be left
for the Muslims. Do the Jewish people truly want to be in this
land? Ask a Jewish person and the answer would be an
emphatic– "Yes!" But the answer is not that simple. For many
centuries the Jewish people moved about the world. They
traveled far and wide, settling and prospering all over the
world. But, at times throughout history, governments became
hostile to their Jewish inhabitants. What resulted was
persecution. The governments of Germany, Spain and Russia,

for example, rounded up their Jewish people and either killed them or forced them to convert or leave. The underlying problem for the Jewish people is their presence as unwanted people in the country where they lived. Having the ability to move and adapt was the hallmark of the Jewish people for such a long time. Now, things have changed. Because of World War II and Hitler's "Final Solution" to exterminate Jews, people of the Jewish faith relocated to a place in Palestine. They call it Israel.

According to the Torah and the Old Testament, the people of Israel entered the kingdom of Egypt thousands of years ago by way of a son of God named Joseph. The brothers of Joseph had become jealous because their father, Jacob, had chosen Joseph over them. One day, one of the brothers lured Joseph away from the house and threw him into a dry well. Later, the brothers decided to sit and have a meal next to the well. A caravan of Ishmaelite came across the brothers eating. One of the brothers had a change of mind and wanted to remove

Joseph from the well. Instead, Joseph was sold to the Ishmaelite for twenty pieces of silver.

From the well in the wilderness, Joseph was sold to a high-ranking member of the Egyptian government named Potiphar. Eventually, he became a courier and steward to the pharaoh. Joseph was a good steward and gained his master's confidence. Then the pharaoh promoted him to be his personal attendant. Joseph was a handsome man and he attracted the attention of the pharaoh's wife. She attempted to seduce Joseph, but Joseph spurned her advances and this made her vengeful. She went to the pharaoh and said Joseph had attempted to sleep with her without her permission. The pharaoh was furious and had Joseph thrown into the dungeon.

While in the dungeon, Joseph met two men who had also worked for the pharaoh. One was a baker and the other a cupbearer. Like Joseph, both had fallen into disfavor and were thrown in prison. One night, the cupbearer had a dream, which he described to Joseph the next morning. In the dream, he saw a vine with three branches; one of the vines had borne grapes.

The cupbearer told Joseph he had crushed the grapes at the bottom of the cup and had given the cup to the pharaoh. Joseph thought about the dream for a moment and then responded that the three vines meant three days. In three days, the pharaoh would pardon the cupbearer, and he would return to work. Joseph asked the cupbearer to remember the dream and tell the pharaoh.

Next, the baker had a dream and asked Joseph to interpret. In the dream, the baker carried three openwork baskets on his head. The top basket was filled with food, and birds were feeding from it. Joseph told him the king would have him killed and his head would be impaled on a stick. Birds would pick the flesh from his skin, Joseph said. After three days, the door to the prison opened and the baker and cupbearer were set free. Both stood before the royal court while a banquet was held. The pharaoh restored the cupbearer to his position and ordered the baker's head impaled on a stick. The cupbearer promptly forgot Joseph's request to tell the dream to the king.

Two years passed, and the pharaoh dreamed he was standing in the Nile River and seven healthy cows came to the bank to drink. Behind those seven came seven more, which were thin and unhealthy. The sick cows stood next to the healthy cows on the bank and swallowed them. When the Pharaoh awoke from his dream, he was frightened but fell asleep again. Next, the king dreamed that seven ears of corn grew on a single stock. The ears were healthy. Then he saw seven more, which looked thin and sickly. The East Wind blew the sick corn, and the healthy corn swallowed them.

The next morning, shaken by the dreams, the king called for his magicians and the wise men to interpret them; however, none of them could. Finally, the cupbearer remembered Joseph the Hebrew in the dungeon and told the pharaoh about him. The king ordered Joseph brought to him. Joseph stood before the pharaoh and listened to him recite the dream. Joseph thought for a moment and replied that the seven cows and seven ears of corn meant seven years. Immediately, there would be seven years of prosperity followed by seven years of hard drought. There would be a famine, which would be severe, and the food supply will fail. Joseph told the pharaoh he would need a man appointed over all the land to take charge and prepare the people for hardship. This man could gather the food and store it for the bitter seven years. He suggested that he, Joseph, was just the man for the job.

The king thought about the request for a moment and then said, "God has granted you the power to see all this. You will be in charge of all my court. You will answer only to me." The king removed the signet ring from his hand and placed it on the hand of Joseph, who was then dressed in fine robes and linen and given a new name, Zaphenath-Paneah. Wherever he went, people kneeled before him and shouted "Abrek!" apparently an honorific title.

For seven years, the kingdom of Egypt enjoyed an abundance of food and wealth. During these years, Joseph gathered food for storage. So much was collected that Joseph ceased counting. At the end of the seven years, a terrible drought began. The people went to the pharaoh and said we need food.

The pharaoh told the people, "Go to Joseph, and he will give you food."

Now, Jacob, the father of Joseph, looked around him and saw that they had nothing to eat. He gathered his sons and said, "Go to Egypt and bring back food so we may live." Jacob's youngest son stayed at home, but the others set out with their camels and baskets. When they arrived in Egypt, Joseph, now the chief overseer of food stores, recognized his half-brothers immediately; however, they did not recognize him. Joseph challenged them, calling them spies.

They answered "No" and told Joseph they were his servants from a land called Canaan. Joseph pretended to doubt them, saying one of them must remain in Egypt. The rest were to go home and bring their father and youngest brother back to Egypt. When the brothers stopped for the night, one of them opened his sack of food bought in Egypt and found, to his surprise, that the sack was filled with the money they had used to pay for the food. They returned home and told their father the story.

Finally that food ran out, and the father once again instructed his sons to go to Egypt. They reminded the father that the overseer would kill them if they did not return with the youngest son, Benjamin. "Take my remaining son and go to Egypt," he told Judah. When the brothers arrived, Joseph was overjoyed at the sight of Benjamin. He instructed the two to sit and eat with him. The next morning, the brothers awoke and set out with their sacks of food. Upon leaving the city, they were stopped by guards, who searched their sacks. Inside one sack was a silver goblet, and the sons fell to their knees pleading their innocence. Joseph had tricked his brothers by having the silver goblet placed in the sack. The guards took Judah and Benjamin back to Joseph, where they again pleaded their innocence. Overcome with emotion, Joseph told them he was the brother they had sold into slavery. He said he had forgiven them and instructed them to return and bring the people of Israel back to Egypt, where they would live in peace. When the people of Israel arrived, they went to the pharaoh, who welcomed them with a gift of the best land in Egypt.

Jacob and his people filled their wagons with gold, clothing and food, and then set off for their new home in Rameses.

The drought worsened, and the people sold their livestock to Joseph in exchange for food. The drought continued, however, and the people become more desperate. To survive, they agreed to become sharecroppers to the king. The famine had become so severe that whole towns from one end of the country to the next were empty of people who became serfs to the king. The only land left untouched was the land owned by priests, who received special immunity. All land sold to the government went to the overseer, Joseph. He let the people stay on their land and gave each person seed to plant. In return, one-fifth of the crop went to the pharaoh. The remaining two-thirds went to the farmer to feed his family.

Time passed, the pharaoh died and a new pharaoh took his place. The new ruler did not look favorably at the arrangement with the people of Israel. He sent taskmasters to make them work harder. The new pharaoh wanted to drive the Jews out of Egypt; however, the people did not want to leave. Instead, they spread out, making it harder for the taskmasters to govern. In retaliation, the king issued an order that midwives must put all newborn Jewish sons to death, but the midwives ignored the order. When the pharaoh learned of this, he sent another order that Jewish male babies would be thrown into the Nile River.

Salvation came in the guise of a beautiful baby born of a man of the tribe of Levi and a Levite woman. The woman hid her son from the taskmasters for three months until she could hide him no more. She then made a basket of reeds, placed the child inside and set it adrift down the river. Downstream, the pharaoh's daughter spotted the baby and brought it to shore. The pharaoh's daughter named her new son, Moses.

Because of his Hebrew nurse, Moses grew up knowing his heritage. One day he went to his people where he witnessed an Egyptian beating a Hebrew. Moses killed him. When a witness informed the king of the murder, Moses fled to the land of Midian. There he came across daughters of the priest of Midian, who were watering their sheep at a watering hole when a shepherd drove them away. Joseph saved the daughters from the shepherd and was rewarded by the priest with the gift of one of his daughters, Zipporah.

As Moses tended his father-in-law's sheep in the wilderness, he rested them in Horeb. On that day, God heard the cries of the Jewish people in Egypt and visited Moses. An angel appeared as a burning bush, and God called out, "Moses!"

"Here I am," said Moses.

"Come, therefore, I will send you to pharaoh, and you shall free my people, the Israelites, from Egypt." God ordered Moses to gather the elders of Israel and tell them, "The Lord, the God of your fathers, the God of Abraham, Isaac and Jacob, has appeared to me and said, 'I am concerned about you and about the way you are being treated in Egypt.' "

The appearance of God and his instructions startled Moses, who asked, "What if they do not believe me?"

"What is in your hand?" asked God.

"A rod."

God told him to cast his rod onto the ground. Moses did so, and his rod turned into a serpent. Moses grabbed the tail of the serpent, and it became a rod once again. This miracle convinced Moses, who took his wife and children to Egypt. Along the way, he joined his brother Aaron, the Levite, in the wilderness.

With Aaron by his side, Moses stood before the pharaoh and said, "Let my people go." Instead, the king turned them away and made life harder for the Jews by increasing the quota of work and decreasing the time they had to do it. God then gave Moses more instructions, so he and Aaron went back to the pharaoh. In the king's presence, Moses struck the Nile River with his rod. The water of the river turned to blood, and the fish died. The stench made the river unbearable and the water undrinkable. However, the pharaoh was not impressed because his magicians had done the same thing.

Moses then held his hands out over the water of the ponds, canals and rivers. Frogs came from the water, covering the land of Egypt. Pharaoh summoned Moses and said, "If you send the frogs away, I will set your people free." The frogs died, leaving a pile of stench in the homes and fields. This hardened the heart of the pharaoh, who refused to let the people go. Once again, Moses went to the pharaoh and said, "Let my people go. If you do not, I will fill the land with insects." So the land was filled with insects. The pharaoh once again summoned Moses, and the insects vanished. Still, the pharaoh refused to release the Jews. Moses went back to God; this time all livestock in Egypt died. The king called his aides, who confirmed that all livestock in Egypt had died, except the livestock of the Jews. The pharaoh refused to budge. Moses took soot from the oven and threw it into the air. The air filled with sand. Men and beasts became sick. Their skins were inflamed with boils. Moses stood before the pharaoh once again and said, "Let my people go or I will pelt the land with hail so hard that no man can survive outside." The Pharaoh refused, and hail pelted Egypt unmercifully.

Finally, after much death and destruction, the pharaoh relented and released the people of Israel. Then he became enraged and ordered his chariots to chase the Jews and strike them down. The chariots caught up with the people of Israel at the sea of reeds (Red Sea). As the chariots were bearing down on the people, Moses stood at the bank and raised his rod. The sea parted and the people of Israel crossed. Just as the Jewish people were reaching the shore, the chariots drove onto the lake bed between the parted waves. Moses raised his rod and released the waters, drowning the soldiers and halting the persecution of the people of Israel by the pharaoh.

Moses took his people to the base of Mount Sinai. He climbed the mountain to receive his instruction from God. Moses did not come down right away. After waiting for forty days and forty nights, Aaron gathered the people and said, "Give me your gold." Believing that Moses had forgotten them, the people of Israel gave Aaron all their gold. He melted it down to make a golden calf idol. The people kneeled, bowed and made sacrifices.

Chapter 7

Come make us a god who will go before us; as for this Moses,
the man who brought us up from the land of Egypt, we do not
know what has become of him

Exodus 31:1 (King James Bible)

Aaron took the calf and proclaimed to the people of Israel,
"This is your new god. This god brought you up from Egypt."
Aaron then built an altar and prayed to the calf. "Tomorrow
shall be a feast for the Lord." The next morning, the people
sacrificed to their new god. From Mountain Sinai, God looked
down upon his people and saw that they had strayed.

The Lord told Moses, "I have seen this people, and behold they
are an obstinate people. Now let me alone that My anger may
burn against them and that I may destroy them; and I will make
you a great nation." Moses intervened, saying, "O Lord why
does your anger burn against your people whom you have

brought out of the land of Egypt with great power and with a mighty hand." God wanted to destroy the people of Israel for their obstinacy, but Moses changed God's mind.

When Moses reached the bottom of the mountain and saw the people of Israel praying to the molten calf, he threw down the tablets, shattering them into pieces. He then took the calf and threw it into the fire. When the gold melted, he ground it into powder and scattered it over the surface of the sea of reeds (Red Sea). He then forced the people to drink water.

Aaron defended himself to his brother, saying, "God's people are prone to evil. They asked me to make them a god from their gold. When I threw it into the fire, the golden calf emerged." The people of Israel were furious at the desecration of their new god, but Moses did not back down. He challenged them, saying, "Whoever did for the Lord, come with me!" The sons of Levi gathered themselves around Moses. Moses told the men of Levi to "walk from gate to gate and slay brother, neighbor and kin." They did as they were told, and 3,000 men of Israel died that day.

Today, in both religious and geographic terms, the nation of Israel is in the center of the war on terror. The radical Muslim does not hate Christians as much as they do Jews; however, America, a Christian state, has chosen to side with Israel. Politics in America are very much pro-Israel. After the death of 6 million Jews in Hitler's concentration camps, many Jews immigrated to the United States, seeking a life away from the politics of Europe. This group has a strong sway in foreign policy towards Israel.

Prior to World War II, the U.S. government was not pro-Jewish. In fact, the government knew about the concentration camps in Germany and did nothing beyond gathering intelligence. They made no move to influence the situation either way. Members of the U.S. government did not understand the inhumanity until top American commanders witnessed it and immigrant Jews flowed into the United States in great numbers. Since then, America has assumed some responsibility for not intervening in the Holocaust until the very end.

Support for the nation of Israel may have also be a manifestation of American forefathers, the Puritans. The Puritans of 1600 were considered ultraconservative in their teaching of the Christian Bible. "Brownists," as they were called, broke from the Protestant group in Britain to seek freedom from the Catholic government. The Puritans compared their migration to America, away from the King of England, to the Jews of Egypt crossing the sea to escape the pharaoh.

America will always be a society based on English adventure and Protestant morals. Every American, whether a recent immigrant or a long-time citizen, possesses these traits of Plymouth's founders. We are a posse of John Smith, adventurer and guide; William Bradshaw, second governor of Plymouth; and the Mayflower Compact, America's first laws. This is who we are. So, today, we live with the memory of the Holocaust and, despite recent grumblings, we continue to stand by Israel.

Israel is a nation of people who have survived despite unimaginable odds. It is a country that was attacked by no less than six nations at once and soundly defeated each one in succession. Could America do this? That would depend on which countries attacked. Even in this day, defending against six countries simultaneously might be beyond our logistical capability. Our country's strength is tied to our ally, Israel. The fall of Israel would put our country in a precarious position, a position that would take many years, trillions of dollars and a great amount of American sacrifice to repair.

Added to the stress of Jews and Muslims occupying the same land is the subject of oil. The West needs oil to run their economies, and the East needs Western technology and management expertise to modernize its countries. Oil serves as the currency of transactions for these goods.

Chapter 8

The British first began extracting oil from the Middle East in 1905 from the Zagros Mountains in Iran. Money to fund the expedition came from private entrepreneurs looking for a wealthy investment. The Iranian government lacked the knowledge to develop the oil; instead, it relied on British private industry to manage the oil fields. Very soon after that, the British government decided it needed oil for its expeditious Navy and assumed greater control of the oil assets from the private firms.

Since the discovery of oil, life for the average Middle Eastern citizen has been tumultuous. Leaders have had to rely on the West for technological know-how to mine the fields. Having these experts and business people in the country has put pressure on the government to make changes at a pace unfamiliar to them. Different approaches to solving the problems were tried. However, rapid change in a society sows feelings of discontent among different groups struggling to adapt. Those most troubled by the change have felt ignored or left behind, unable to catch up in the whirlwind of innovation.

Distribution of resources is the main cause of friction. Investors are primarily worried about the bottom line. In response, leadership becomes rigid and less forgiving in enforcing its business plan, and this has led to state-sponsored human-rights violations. Governments struggle to make changes in their own country and have to deal with neighboring states who want a piece of the economic action. Like their neighbors, these neighboring countries with old animosities are keen to get rich. Western governments have used this desire to their advantage by manipulating insecurities that keep people from uniting under a common cause. This divide-and-conquer technique, in the past, has been applied by Iran to isolate Israel from the Western governments of the United States, Great Britain and France.

The Iranians did not invent divide-and-conquer diplomacy. They learned it from their British managers who first used it against the Iranian people to keep national alliances from forming against the oil companies. Prior to WWI, both Russia and Great Britain had enormous presence in the oil fields of Iran. Britain staked its territory in the southern half of the country, while Russia staked its claim to the north. In the middle were the Iranian people who were overwhelmingly afraid that communist Russians were about to take over their country. Britain capitalized on this by posing as the answer to the communist problem. The British could help keep the menacing red tide at bay in exchange for promises.

The end of World War I found Russia's Tsar Nicholas facing what he thought was a minor rebellion on the home front. In February 1917, female factory workers celebrating International Women's Day in Petrograd, modern-day St. Petersburg, spilled into the streets in protest over food shortages. Russia had been experiencing riots before this. Initially, it seemed like just another typical riot, so the government was slow to react. The Russian people, however, had had enough of not having enough, and the "February Revolution" quickly spread. Striking workers took over the railway station, which the government normally used to transport soldiers to stop rioters. They then took over the entire city, including army artillery supplies at Petrograd. The chaos forced Nicholas to abdicate his throne, and his family to become prisoners. On July 17, 1918, Bolshevik troops shot the Tsar, his wife and his children in the Ipatiev house basement in Ekaterinburg, Russia.

Vladimir Lenin and his Russian Communist Party (CPSU) were an aggressive political party, which practiced professional politics. This means the CPSU party worked full time to push its agenda, unlike other political organizations whose members organized on a part-time basis. The CPSU took control by rushing in and taking advantage of the confused situation, effectively pushing all political opposition aside. On Feb. 26, 1921, Lenin ordered Russian soldiers home from Iran.

When World War II started, both Britain and Russia found themselves on the bayonet end of the German Army. The two enemies became allies to stop German aggression. In 1941, just two months after Germany invaded Russia, both Britain and Russia moved to occupy Iran. Meanwhile Japan bombed Pearl Harbor in Hawaii.

The bombing of Pearl Harbor brought an economically depressed but still-vigorous America into the fight. America signed Lend-Lease agreements with both countries and immediately began shipping large amounts of combat equipment to Europe and Eurasia. The British immediately requested 30,000 American troops for logistical help in transporting Lend-Lease war material from ports in southern Iran to Russia. From then on, Americans would be a major political presence in Middle Eastern politics.

In 1946, Russia withdrew its troops from Iran after getting oil concessions from the Iranian government. The end of the war brought more oil investment and exploration in Iran and Saudi Arabia. America invested a lot of money into Iran, a large and still-underdeveloped country. In the end, all the oil, sweat and tears invested into Iran came down to a single event that would change American politics.

Before Reza Shah Pahlavi (the Shah of Iran), there was Dr. Mohammed Mossedagh, prime minister of Iran from 1951 to 1953. He held power over his citizens, but the British held power over him. The British wanted to control the oil fields of Persia. Mossedagh wanted to control his own people and to kick the British out.

Reza was optimistic about his country. He wanted to make his agrarian people into a regional power. He disliked the British, but without their money and help, he never would be able to achieve his dream. The country the shah disliked most was the one that was keeping him in power.

At one time, the United Kingdom had an empire stretching from North America to Africa, India and Australia. Subsequent wars had changed all this. By the end of World War II, the British Empire was a mere shadow of the old. The British

Empire, which "the sun never set upon," had been slimmed down in size. Still, in the Persian Gulf, the Royal Navy was the law. Britain got what it wanted by pressuring local governments by use of gunboat diplomacy. The omnipresent British Navy acted as a reminder that it was never far away and could react if needed.

All this changed in 1968 when Britain announced it would withdrawal its forces east of the Suez Canal. This left a power vacuum that the Chinese and Russians hoped to step into. To counter this aggression, Britain proposed an Arab Federation called the "Trucial States," led by Iran. However, other Arab states feared the growing influence of Iran and turned against the idea. The Trucial State Federation collapsed.

Impatient with having the British and Americans in his country, Mossedagh nationalized the oil industry. This placed all equipment and profits of the foreign oil companies under government control. The British and Americans countered his decision by bringing a coup against Mossedagh. In 1953, the Reza seized control of the government in a bloodless coup, which he almost lost. During the coup, the Reza fled the country because it looked like the coup had failed; however, large protests supported by CIA money took to the streets. Less than one week after his retreat to Rome, Reza returned and took control of the country, jailing Mossedagh.

Reza was a man much like Napoleon, a successful military officer in battle who believed in strict control. Many in his country thought him to be a British agent. However, he disliked the British and preferred to do business with the United States because it had lots of money and was far, far away, not like the British.

From then on, American money flowed into Iran. The Iranian people were glad the British were gone, but the Americans had simply replaced the British. The people were becoming frustrated, particularly with the CIA.

With Reza in power, the American government was more than willing to give money. In the 1950s, President Eisenhower extended two grants totaling $70 billion. In exchange for the grants, American oil companies received 40 percent control of the Iran oil industry. Profits were split evenly, 50-50, with American oil companies getting one-half and Iran the other. For Reza, it was a much better deal than the deal made with Great Britain. To the CIA, it kept the Reza where they could keep an eye on him.

To strengthen the government's power, Iran built a large military complex. An increase in military spending usually brings with it local jobs, which, in turn, fuel taxes and the economy; however, much of the country's population was still agrarian. Most families farmed and had little use for education or trade skills. So American workers worked instead to build and maintain the infrastructure. Of course, this had the opposite effect of what was intended. The village poor remained poor while a very select group of citizens became wealthy.

The CIA also developed a secret intelligence agency known and feared by the people called SAVAK, Sazman-e Etela' at Va Amniyat-e Keshvar. By 1950, the Reza had established almost complete control over a population known for its many opposition groups. In 1954, the Reza purged his military, ordering the execution of six hundred military officers with alleged ties to the Tudeh, a pro-Soviet communist movement. Eventually, political reforms were made; but, even after reform, the brutal methods of the SAVAK continued. The SAVAK would become the No. 1 reason for the people turning against the government and for the rise of a shadowy figure called Ayatollah Ruhollah Khomeini.

In 1958, a general named Qarani came close to succeeding in a plot to overthrow Reza. He had a large number of officers to back him, but it failed. Finally, dissatisfaction by the general population, repeated coup attempts and pressure from the American government persuaded Reza to institute reforms called the "White Revolution." The idea was to take land owned by the minority upper class and redistribute it to the poor. It also nationalized the forest and pasture lands. The change was to happen "through no disorder and no bloodshed." The political party system also changed from being a uni-party to a dual party system. State-owned factories were sold to private investors. The new change in electoral law would allow women's rights and a literacy corps that would lead to increased education. Changes took place with the speed of a rolling locomotive, and the popularity of Reza rose.

In 1953, Great Britain organized a federation of seven Middle Eastern states to bring peace and stability to the area. The understanding was that the states would have semi-independence, and Great Britain would provide for their military defense and foreign politics. In 1971, most of these individual states formed a union to become one country called the United Arab Emirates, which replaced the now defunct Trucial States Federation.

The collapse of the Trucial States Federation and birth of the United Arab Emirates must have been a disappointment to Reza, who had wanted to make Iran the regional power. Iran had been importing large numbers of weapons from America, which gave it great strength against outside hostilities. However, the rapid growth of the military had a negative effect within the country's borders. Many Iranians living in the country remained poor, without good sanitation and medical care. They were under-educated, which prevented them from finding jobs in the modern cities. Nevertheless, Reza began exporting weapons and military supervisors outside the Middle East. He sent weapons to Somalia, a country at war with its neighbor, Ethiopia. Iran became the largest weapons supplier to Mohammad Siad Barre, president of Somalia. Eventually, the presence of the CIA, the brutality of the SAVAK trained by the CIA and fiscal corruption would culminate in the storming of the American Embassy.

Reza used his compatriots' fear of the CIA as his own bully pulpit, which increased negative feelings toward Americans. Corruption within the government was everywhere. Reforms instituted failed because the government did not rein in corrupt government officials. It was much easier for Reza to use the CIA to play off the fears of the people than to control his government. These fears were not something born of the peoples' imagination. The British had used secretive intelligence methods against the people of Iran before the Americans.

Through graft, Reza kept an imbalance between the haves and the have-nots. Government officials demanded bribes to issue contracts and to do regular day-to-day services. Because of graft, government employees did well financially while private industry suffered. This gave rise to a new middle class, people with government jobs living in cities. Those living in the country were left out of such wealth. The government chose to harbor its resources in city development with the idea that more people would gravitate away from the rural, less productive lifestyle. However, people moving from the suburbs to the city arrived with little or no education and thus failed to find work.

In time, these problems magnified, and the gap between the haves and have-nots widened. Modernization did benefit a large portion of the country, and, on more than one occasion, Reza did institute programs to assist people living in the rural areas. Although grand in size, these plans never achieved their intended goals. Improper planning, graft, poor management, over-ambitious planning and bad oversight put more money in the hands of unscrupulous officials.

Graft and persecution by the SAVAK became an everyday occurrence. This was not a secret to the American government. President Jimmy Carter put increased pressure on the king to change his ways. However, Reza and those around him were making a lot of money from corruption and arms sales, and he resisted making necessary changes. Finally, Reza was forced to act because his ability to influence the Iranian people was slipping away. He ordered the SAVAK to cease the torture of dissidents, and he pardoned some political prisoners. He changed policy to deal with the graft, which had bottlenecked government services. By this time, however, the damage had been already done, and many previously silenced voices of opposition now surfaced.

Many different groups with different agendas became increasingly vocal. A lesser-known group of Shia Muslims led by the influential but brutal Ayatollah Khomeini suddenly appeared as a leader among the opposition. Fed up with the savage treatment of the SAVAK and government corruption, protesters took to the streets, angry and looking for change. By mid-1978, a large anti- Reza movement was surging forward. People from all walks of life, including students, business owners, intellectuals and the country poor, marched to a unifying chant: "Down with the Shah and his oppressive corrupt rule … Long live Khomeini, Islam, democracy, freedom and equality." The protest and anti-government activity had been building for months until one morning when 37,000 oil workers began a limited strike. The planned short-term strike became prolonged, forcing an absolute work stoppage.

Fearing the worst, Reza imposed martial law in twelve cities and admitted that mistakes had been made. He appointed Gen. Gholam Azhar to run the military-controlled government. Years of suppression had made the people bitter beyond forgiveness. The more Reza retreated from power, the harder Khomeini and his devoted supporters pushed. Momentum continued to escalate until millions of people were taking to the streets of Tehran in protest.

On Nov. 4, 1979, 450 people, mostly students, approached the gates of the American Embassy shouting, "Death to the Shah. Death to Carter. Death to America." Just two weeks prior, the Shah had left the country, allegedly to seek cancer treatment in the U.S. That morning Moorhead Kennedy, senior diplomat and Harvard graduate, stood at his second-story office at the American Embassy, Tehran. He looked beyond the embassy wall at the demonstrators, wondering what it would be like to die. Three hours later, a Marine guard burst open the office door, shouting, "There is a break-in!"

Iran began as a military investment and ended as a military failure. However, on the other side of the Persian Gulf in Saudi Arabia, business was booming. Large construction corporations and weapons were flowing into the kingdom. Cities, roads and ports were popping up out of nowhere, replacing the empty desert with a modern society.

Chapter 9

Today, Saudi Arabia is one of the richest oil nations in the world. Its production of oil actually began as a search for gold. King Abdul Aziz ibn Saud of Saudi Arabia needed money and hired a prospector, Karl Twitchell, from a California company named SoCal, later known as Chevron. Twitchell searched the scorching desert for gold and water and came up empty-handed and out of money. He convinced the king he could get more investors if he searched for oil.

In the 1930s, Saudi Arabia was a land of Bedouin tribes roaming the vast desert plains, moving from trading town to trading town. The mode of transportation was the camel, so trying to convince the king he needed oil was not easy. Finally, ibn Saud gave permission, and money from investors began pouring in. Looking for oil was difficult, and business decisions were made in the moment without the benefit of lawyers. The relationship between the king and explorers was tested at times, but common interest in money and oil kept it together.

For the king, losing control over the exploration was something he feared most. The Saudi government had watched the drama unfolding in Iran and wished to stay away from coups and demonstrations. Keeping the tribes of Arabia at peace was enough of a challenge. The king feared that demonstrations could result into the loss of the kingdom itself.

For the oil companies, negotiating with the House of Saud was tough. The House of Saud feared losing control, so it kept negations close to the heart. Before signing contracts, family members often were brought into negotiations. The Saudis needed time to get to know the Americans, and this could take months or years. They measured success by the value of the relationship. Since the Americans measured success by production, they were frustrated by these business deals.

American companies were expected to invest in the local economy. When they constructed roads, schools, housing and infrastructure for oil production, they had to hire local workers. Anything the local people needed was provided by the company. The most prominent company in Saudi Arabia, Aramco (Arabian American Oil Co.), came from a conglomerate of oil companies: SoCal of California; and Texaco, Mobil and Standard of New Jersey. Taking oil from the ground was extremely lucrative and also built the nation's roads, schools, electricity and even whole cities.

Once the projects were completed, the Saudi government wanted to assume control for themselves; however, Saudi workers did not have the education or training. In light of this, the Americans remained in the country to manage operations.

On March 3, 1938, after drilling six dry holes, SoCal struck it rich. The first oil strike was in Dhahran. Dammam No. 7 produced 32 million barrels of oil before finally shutting down in 1982.

World War II was a turning point in American-Saudi relations. An Italian military plane on a mission to bomb a British installation dropped its bomb on Dhahran, killing nobody and inflicting only minor damage. However, the bombing set into motion the American government's deepening involvement with the House of Saud. In February 1945, the warship USS Quincy took on forty-eight members of the House of Saud along with its sheep and tents, which were tethered on the ship's deck. President Franklin Roosevelt and the King reportedly got along splendidly. They exchanged presents, and a lasting friendship between the two countries was cemented.

The year 1949 was a banner year for Aramco. Four new booming oil fields, Abqaiq, Qatif, Ain Dar and Fadhili, were discovered. To transport all this new oil, a pipeline had to be built. The line ran from Dhahran to the Mediterranean Sea and spawned a new company, the Trans-Arabian Pipeline Consortium, or Tapline for short. The pipeline crossed 1,400 miles of empty desert and ended in Sidon, Lebanon. It was privately financed and required the employment of 16,000 men with 350,000 pounds of pipes, vehicles, food and supplies. All this was done by Bechtel Corp. of San Francisco. If Aramco was the brains, then Bechtel was the brawn. From then on, Bechtel Corp. built all the large construction the kingdom needed done. Bechtel built ports, railroads, schools, factories, airports and the entire city of Al Jubail, a port city used to land millions of tons of supplies and personnel for the First Gulf War.

As time went on, the Saudi Arabian government and Aramco became one entity. Maps developed by the company were used de facto to settle border disputes. When the kingdom needed troops moved into troubled spots, trucks from Aramco moved them. The company also provided textbooks for children, drugs for malaria eradication and asphalt for roads. In 1947, Crown Prince Saud took a $682,000 trip to America paid for by Aramco. Saudi Arabia was undergoing a major change. Just a few years before, most of the population raised goats, pitched tents and rode camels from watering hole to watering hole. New ideas brought by Americans began to cause friction in the local population and government. Large, modern, westernized compounds were built to separate nationals from foreigners. So long as neither alcohol nor religion was brought to the locals, the government was willing to ignore what went on inside the compound walls. The compounds, Dhahran, Abqaiq, Ras Tanura and Udhailiyah, had all the amenities of a Western city. They had golf courses, theaters, baseball, sailboats, tennis, social groups and so on. Those inside lived a structured life, and everyone knew everyone else. The rules of the compound forbade those living outside to socialize with those on the inside. Some people adjusted to their new surroundings and became part of the community; those who did not soon left.

The Westerners were not the only ones adjusting. The Saudi people employed by the oil companies had to learn new ways of living. Before, individuals answered mostly to themselves, keeping time by the rise and fall of the sun. A man's self-worth was measured in flocks of animals and the number of wives he possessed. Imams (Islamic leaders) were on hand to give advice according to the Koran. The Saudi people knew nothing of living a structured life under the leadership of a manager. Often, citizen workers new to the oil company arrived and left work whenever they wanted. The idea of working by a clock had to be taught and reinforced. Most of the workers were uneducated, but they had to learn if they wanted to rise to management positions and earn more money.

Westerners living in the compounds made more money and had better living conditions. This was always a source of conflict with the local workers. The first workers' strike in 1945 was modest compared with Western riots. It was more like a public gathering in which the workers turned and left the scene upon the arrival of troops. The idea of a riot was conversation enough; to actually have one was a big step. Each time workers rioted, the government would force the oil company to make changes. One of these changes was to send young Saudi men to America for university schooling. The idea was to make manager material out of young Saudi men who could rise up through the ranks of the workers. Educating Saudi workers came as a result of workers' complaints that they wanted to live a Western lifestyle but were not being paid equivalent wages.

American managers did not block the promotion of workers, but many of the uneducated workers resisted Western ideals of workplace etiquette. For some, going to the U.S. was an experience of a lifetime. For others, it was an emotional corruption that sickened them, pushing them to the edge of fundamentalism.

Even though the workers received more of what they wanted, it was never enough. Ultimately, what they wanted was to be nearly like the American and foreign workers who came into their country.

They wanted the cars, homes, pay and lifestyle that they eventually rebelled against anyway. Another problem was the importation of lower-skilled foreign workers from such places as the Philippines, Thailand and Africa. Since most people in Saudi Arabia were supported by the government and did not work, these foreign workers were imported for many years.

The foreign workers were housed inside camps where officials could keep an eye on them, and they were treated poorly for the most part. These workers brought unresolved nationalistic issues from their home country, which increased tension.

With an imported work force came riots, which became exceedingly violent, demanding and commonplace. In May 1953, foreign workers in Saudi Arabia petitioned for better housing, wages, transportation and schools for the children. The petition set the stage for a showdown with government policy. A group of workers entered a meeting with officials and shouted demands at the commission. This was going too far. The workers and citizens were allowed to question the House of Saud but not to challenge it directly. The workers took to the streets where they rioted outside the American Dhahran Air Force base, stoning and burning a bus. The response by the government was swift and decisive. It sent in 2,000 troops, who arrested hundreds of protesters and deported others. This petition was a direct challenge to the government of Saudi Arabia, which would not allow a direct challenge.

The close partnership between Aramco and the House of Saud was never the same after the riot. On payday, the strike ended, and government troops went back to their barracks. Henceforth, all strikes were outlawed and the strike leaders were banished to their faraway villages for ten years. Being banished meant not having a job, as villages were miles and miles away from employment in the big cities. Twenty years later, Aramco would become nationalized, though most of the American managers remained.

The end of World War II heralded new changes to the Middle East. One of these was a new country in the land of Palestine. This new country, Israel, became an immediate thorn in the side of the rest of the Middle East. On June 5, 1967, the neighboring states of Egypt and Syria attacked Israel in a pincher-like movement of attack. The attack took the forces of Israel completely by surprise. Israel, however, successfully crushed its opponents one by one, pushing the attackers out. Winning the war meant adding new territory, which meant taking control of the holy city of Jerusalem and adding one million new citizens for the state. This was not just a defeat to the armies of Egypt and Syria, but also defeat in the minds of the rest of the Middle East, including Saudi Arabia. The 1967 Six-Day War was a humiliating loss for the Arabs. Israel, the sworn enemy of the Koran, trounced Muslim forces. The Saudi government, or members within the Saudi government, wanted to show support to its Muslim brethren who fought in the Six-Day War. It also wanted to send a message of protest to the Americans, who supported Israel. Students in Saudi Arabia were organized and forced to attack the American Consulate in a riot that appeared half-hearted and rehearsed. Within a half hour, government troops were marched in. The commander fired six shots in the air, and everyone went home.

By 1949, the House of Saud was making billions. Taking and spending the money was no problem, but the House of Saud knew nothing of fiscal management. This became a concern for the American government, which feared that the House of Saud was fast approaching monetary collapse. Living standards were rising and the rest of the country was moving forward.

Empty expanses of sand were now covered by modern cities with all the latest amenities: sewers, electricity, schools, hospitals and shopping malls. Before the oil money, change had happened at a slow, measured walk; now the pace was dizzying. Those who had grown up as livestock farmers could not keep up. Members of the royal family were spending money faster than it was coming in while regular citizens continued to live in tents or rundown homes.

In 1958, Crown Prince Faisal, appointed prime minister, audited the kingdom's ledger and discovered that 60 percent of all revenue from oil production went to members of the royal family. The kingdom's bank account contained a mere $100. The country's financial system was in far worse shape than anybody imagined. People had assumed that there would always be more money.

After other countries denied loans to Saudi Arabia, Faisal turned to President Truman for help. Truman went to the U.S. State Department with the request, and international finance expert Arthur Young started the herculean task of organizing the kingdom's finances. Young accepted the task, always keeping with him a letter of resignation if he did not get his way. The letter, kept in his front pocket, became tattered, but remained unused. Organizing the country's financial system was no easy task. Young had to build it from the ground up.

Until 1963, the kingdom of Saudi Arabia was completely centralized. All decision-making came from the king or members of the royal family. In the end, it was only the empty bank account that inspired the royal family to change. Everything from banking, judicial matters, transportation, armed forces and sanitation had to be organized. In 1963, the American Ford Foundation signed an agreement with the Saudi government to provide personnel and training to staff the new Saudi government.

The foundation thought it had agreed to work as an adviser to the Saudis, who would eventually take charge of the government. However, the king decided the foundation's role was to carry out the orders of the king. The government spent a large amount of money constructing modern buildings and an infrastructure. The king had the best and most up-to-date Western technology; however, when it came time to operate the new infrastructure, the country did not have enough trained or educated people who could understand the complex machinery.

Recruiting Saudi citizens was a difficult task. They did not care for employment in public service. Service to oneself was priority. The experience proved difficult for members of the American Ford Foundation, which reported that "the average civil servant is poorly educated, incompetent, and underemployed, given to corruption and not wanting to participate in low-level functions." Saudi citizens viewed manual labor as something below a person's status. As a solution, the country imported thousands of workers from Africa and Asia as manual labor.

Initially, the government did not practice social infrastructure planning. To the Saudis, communists practiced planning, which went against Muslim religious teaching. Prior to the formation of government services, if a hospital was needed, it was built, without planning. Now, citizens had to be taught rudimentary working skills before they could begin employment. Progress was slow, but eventually a complete civil service system was up and running on its own.

The large Ford Foundation agency, which had been working all over the country to create an efficient social service system, was downsized into a single apartment in Riyadh. Then, in January 1977, word came from the royal family that the foundation, after being reduced in size, was to be closed within the week.

The 1970s were a particularly busy time for Saudi Arabia and Aramco. The demand for oil was skyrocketing. The oil manufacturing and the transportation system could not keep up with production. Thirty thousand new workers from Third World countries like Pakistan, India, and the Philippines came to Saudi Arabia to fill labor needs. Professional engineers and managers from America and Europe took jobs to build and run machinery. The kingdom embarked on an unprecedented building spree, constructing new schools, hospitals, ports, pipelines and roads. The military received brand-new, state-of-the-art F-15 fighter jets, naval ships, tanks and barracks facilities.

Businessmen came from all over the world to sign contracts with Saudi business owners. The large new hotels ran out of room, so visiting business people hired cab drivers to drive them around the city at night with the air conditioning on so they could sleep. The financial system handling all this money was under enormous strain. Bribes, which had always been a part of life, reached stratospheric heights. The nation's fair practices arbitration system that once settled business disputes was so overwhelmed that cases often were not heard for years. Saudi businessmen, if they desired, could choose not to pay their contractors.

There was an understanding in Saudi Arabia regarding Christians and Jews. The country simply did not tolerate Jews. The government tolerated Christians only so long as they did not practice Christianity in the open or attempt to convert Saudi citizens. The policy on religion worked without significant problems until the First Gulf War (1991) when the influx of American military personnel overwhelmed the reclusive country. As a gesture of gratitude toward Americans, American Muslim soldiers were allowed to make the religious pilgrimage to Mecca, called Hajj. This was an important step in Eastern-Western relations. For the first time, Saudi Arabia recognized there were people of Muslim belief outside the Middle East. The pilgrimages symbolized the recognition of people of Muslim faith all around the world.

The massive air and sealift of American troops into Saudi Arabia settled the question of American Jews in the kingdom. Since the U.S. military did not deselect Jews from the ranks when deploying to the First Gulf War, the law forbidding Jews from entering the kingdom became a technicality. The government simply listed all Jewish service members entering the country as monotheists, not Jews.

Unfortunately, this policy became a rallying cry for radical Muslims like Osama bin Laden. For years, the topic of Jews in the kingdom was a subject of the strictest taboo. If American companies wanted to do business in the country, they could never send Jews to work in the oil fields. When King Saud made a trip to America on Feb. 13, 1962, for a meeting with President Kennedy, Kennedy began by first apologizing for speaking of the matter. Then he forced the issue of Jews traveling to the kingdom.

Up to this point, the kingdom practiced a "do not ask -do not tell" policy for military members. If the military sent people to repair a plane, then the kingdom did not ask their religion and the military did not tell. After his meeting with Kennedy, Saud permitted Jewish Secretary of State Henry Kissinger and members of his staff to enter Saudi Arabia for talks.

Chapter 10

The Iran-Iraq War (September 1980-August 1988) went badly for Saddam Hussein. As it turned out, he was not the Napoleon he thought he was. A war that should have been a win for Iraq became its undoing. Iranian child soldiers using Japanese World War II banzai-charge tactics pushed the Iraqi army back deep inside Iraqi territory. The American government, which had been supplying weapons to both sides, decided to intercede on Saddam's behalf and supply him with intelligence, training and chemical weapons of mass destruction. Saddam used the chemical weapons to beat back the hordes of Iranian soldiers and then turned them on his own people, the Kurds. World leaders, including the American government, protested Saddam's act of genocide. However, the American government continued to supply him with WMDs; otherwise, they feared losing influence in Middle Eastern policy and, of course, losing the money.

While Iraq was busy with its war, Kuwait began to take an interest in the Rumailia oil field in Iraq, twenty miles from Kuwait. The profit made from mining the field would be significant to either country. For Iraq, it could mean the difference between paying its war loans or being forever in debt to America and Europe for weapons. To Kuwait, it would mean more money for its burgeoning welfare society that provided free health care, education, and housing to its citizens.

Iraq was embroiled in war with Iran and too busy to protect its oil resources. The Kuwaiti Army and oil wildcatters crossed the border, driving 900 miles inside Iraq and seizing control of the Rumailia field. Saddam's first response was to open negotiations with America and Kuwait to reclaim at least part of the land; however, the American government refused to negotiate.

Though it shouldn't have, the attack on Kuwait came as a big surprise to Saudi Arabia. A potential invader was sitting on its border, and neither the royal family nor the government knew how to respond. Weapons supplied by the U.S. to Saudi Arabia were of excellent quality, but the Iraqi army was much larger and already mobilized.

The royal family and government officials debated how to manage the situation. Opinion within the family was split. One side wanted to do what the royal family had always done—buy off the enemy. The other half wanted to settle the crisis diplomatically through the Arab League. Osama bin Laden offered 100,000 *Mujahedin* fighters on a faith-based—"God is with us so we will prevail"—attack to drive the invading Iraqis out of Kuwait. King Fahd took charge and, instead, made an agreement with the American government. His conditions were that American soldiers were to abide by Islamic law, built no permanent bases and leave when asked. When Defense Secretary Dick Cheney assured Fahd that the American government would respect the rules set forth, the king gave a swift and final yes.

America responded by sending planes, ships, tanks and Marines to the Persian Gulf. Men, women and material from the U.S., Asia and Europe began to flood into the kingdom at a pace never experienced by the Saudi people. This influx of Western people with their western ideas set off a cultural chain reaction from which the country is still recovering.

The rigid religious right went on the offensive criticizing the government, in prayer. Prayer is the most efficient way of communicating ideas and news to the Muslim population. Clerics record the message and then broadcast at prayer time over public loudspeakers. Individuals pass the recording onto friends in villages where they then play them on recorders.

The people of Saudi Arabia viewed its government as being soft, corrupt and incapable of dealing with the complicated Iraqi-Kuwaiti situation on its own. However, to Muslims, Saudi Arabia is "the kingdom," the holy place that is Muslim. The Muslims are the defenders of the Koran. For Christians to come into the land of Mohammed to defend it was abhorrent, worse than that—treason. However, the government knew it could not take on the Iraqi army alone; something like that could bring down the government. Its only alternative was to station American soldiers on its soil.

Fahd invited Americans into his country to defend against Saddam. To fend off his critics, Fahd also sided with national religious conservatives who wanted to crack down on all things un-Islamic. Saudi Arabia is a country with two police forces. One force enforces criminal law such as murder and theft. The second is the Mutawa'in, religious police, which enforces the religious laws of the Koran. At the beginning of Operation Desert Shield, with the build-up of coalition forces, the religious police routinely seized its female military drivers until ordered by the king to redeploy to the south of the country, away from coalition forces.

The fact that American military women drove vehicles was not a secret to the women of Saudi Arabia. In fact, it inspired female Arabs to exercise their opinions through action. On Nov. 6, 1990, forty-five female professors from Riyadh took to the streets in a convoy of fourteen cars. Some even removed their headscarves and were photographed by the *New York Times.* The government could not ignore this very public display of protest by female subjects of the kingdom, so the

Mutawa'in scorned the women in public. The women and their husbands lost their jobs and their right to travel outside the country. Not having a job or the ability to leave the country meant either living in poverty or from the generosity of relatives. The reaction by the government was brutal, but retribution taken by the private citizenry was worse. They humiliated the women by publicly posting the women's names, workplaces and home addresses, and people went to their homes to confront them. The women lost their jobs and the vital support of their community.

The First Gulf War, although a success for the coalition, had left the royal family in a vulnerable position. Previously, the royal family kept the peace with payoffs. It could afford to do this because the kingdom had a flourishing budget. Now, after the war, it was in debt up to 55 percent of its gross national product. Without payoffs by the government, people like Osama bin Laden would cease to yield their activities. This left the radicals free to exert their influence like never before. The king knew he had to act quickly. He jailed many of the hardliner Islamists and imams to quiet them. Osama bin Laden, a member of the House of Saud, was exiled to Sudan. At the same time, the government also extended an olive branch to appease the Mutawa'in by increasing its authority. Fahd reintroduced laws called the Basic Law of Government. Under these laws, the king reaffirmed his right to rule, which meant absolute obedience from his subjects, according to the law of the land—the Koran. In addition, he introduced and appointed sixty members to the Consultative Counsel. This legal body would review policy, nominate members to the council and organize policy-making committees. Though the king's actions looked as though they affirmed the laws of Islam, they merely affirmed the king's right of absolute rule. The changes did little to convince the male population that any real change had taken place.

Each country within the Middle East has its own individual issues, but most share the same single problem—too many men and not enough women. This imbalance has led to a highly educated ambitious male population with no jobs and few opportunities. With time on their hands, many of these young men have joined radical groups to prove themselves and to force change.

The Middle East is ruled by three countries: Saudi Arabia has the most oil, making it the real regional power. Israel has an army known for crushing its opponents and holds the nuclear card. The United States acts as godfather, granting favors in return for friendship. Together these three countries will decide the fate of the Middle East.

Chapter 11

Politics is a matter of convenience. An ally of today is tomorrow's enemy and yesterday's warming partner. The invasion of Iran by Iraq was acceptable and even encouraged. When Iraqi forces turned and invaded Kuwait in 1990, two of the most powerful families in the world, the House of Bush and House of Saud, counterattacked in a war leading up to the invasion of Iraq.

Following the invasion of Kuwait by Iraqi forces, the American media went into overtime, showing to the American people a picture of extreme Iraqi aggression. A mysterious fifteen-year-old girl rescued from the clutches of Iraqi intelligence went before the Congressional Human Rights Caucus. She told a tragic story of Iraqi troops invading Kuwait City, snatching hospital incubators and leaving newborn babies to die on the floor. The story ran in the press hundreds of times, describing

Iraqi soldiers committing despicable acts to a peace-loving people of a tiny nation.

The story, however, was a media campaign waged by the politically perceptive public relations firm Hill & Knowlton. Its services were paid by a call-to-action group funded by the government of Kuwait called, Citizens for a Free Kuwait. The Pentagon aired intelligence footage of invading Iraqi troops poised on the Saudi-Kuwaiti border ready to attack Saudi Arabia.

The American people were hungry for information about the war. They supported the people of Kuwait by wearing T-shirts and putting bumper stickers on their cars. The American people relied on their government to tell them the truth. What they got was an extended Hollywood epic shown to them free of charge. The "brave" fifteen-year-old girl pulled from the ring of devastation actually was the daughter of the Kuwait ambassador to the United States. Nobody knew of her whereabouts during the invasion months of August and September 1990, but it is unlikely that she witnessed Iraq soldiers committing the atrocities she described. An investigation conducted by the New York-based human rights group Middle East Watch found the story of babies pulled from their incubators to be false. An interview of Kuwaiti doctors by ABC News reporter John Martin confirmed that the babies found dead did, in fact, perish, but not because of Iraqi soldiers. Hospital staff abandoned the hospital during the invasion leaving patients and infants to look after themselves. The 250,000 crack Iraqi troops that were positioned on the border to invade Saudi Arabia never materialized. Satellite photos taken by Soviet satellites showed no activity of troops on the border.

All this started long before the invasion of Iran or Kuwait. It really started in Texas where the relationship of the Saud and Bush families first began. Former President George Herbert Walker Bush was a two-term congressman from Texas, oil businessman and director of the CIA. He attended Yale University and was a decorated World War II air combat pilot, having flown 58 missions over the Pacific. His son, George

Bush Jr. holds a similar pedigree. He attended Yale, became a fighter pilot and entered the oil business, though with less luck. He served in the Texas Air National Guard as a fighter pilot with the 111th Fighter Interceptor Squadron, nicknamed the "Champagne Squadron." Sons from prominent families could join and serve their time in this squadron without the fear of deployment to Southeast Asia.

Here, Bush Jr. met fellow squadron member James Bath, who became a point man between the Saudi royal family and the politically connected American *uberclass*. The royal family hired Bath to fly a newly purchased aircraft from Texas to Saudi Arabia. Members of the royal family were flying enthusiasts. Many held pilot licenses and were known for taking holidays with a large staff to gamble in Monaco and other places. Over time, Texas became a second home for them.

The Saudi royal family first came to power in 1747 when the country was made up of different tribes vying for power. One clan, Al-Saud, led by Adb al-Aziz Al Saud, fought its way up the power chain by defeating its enemies. The country's first government was formed when a member of the Saud clan married a member of the ibn Abd al-Wahhab clan. To keep power within the family, it was decided that governance would be handed down from one family member to the next.

The Saud clan practices a very strict form of Islam called "Wahhabism," named after the ibn Abd al-Wahhab clan. By creating this alliance, the tribe became more powerful than its enemies. It forced each enemy tribe it encountered to submit to the strict practice of Wahhabism. Those who refused found themselves under continued attacks, which sapped the strength of the tribe until it could no longer protect itself. In the end, the power of Al-Saud and ibn Abd al-Wahhab overcame all resistance and conquered the remaining desert tribes.

The discovery of oil in the 1930s was a boon to the royal family, which was originally looking for water. The king had hired a Western geologist from California to find water for his people; however, once oil was discovered, the search for water was postponed until the first oil strike and the construction of a pipeline. Ultimately, the royal family became rich beyond its wildest dreams. No records were kept on money made or money spent, but most of the country's revenues went to ruling family members who bought planes and homes. They flew from country to country with large staffs on a Boeing 747. Each member of the family received a monthly allowance. King Saud married one hundred women, his palace cost $13 billion and he regularly spent hundreds of thousands of dollars in a single evening of gambling. The stories of excess are legend. The king was known to have spent $8 million on himself and his entourage during a night of gambling. This traveling party was made up of eight planes, five of them Boeing 747s; four hundred retainers' two hundred tons of baggage and twenty-five Rolls Royce limos for ground transport.

The money and excess of the royal family eventually led to the corruption of the government. Many times, members of the family who found themselves in jail simply walked out with their crimes forgiven. No judge would risk his own head by convicting a member of the family. The decadence and overindulgence in Western culture, a sin in the Arabic world, became a way of life for some within the family, though it was the opposite for others. Gambling, sex and the use of profanity are against the laws of the Koran. To the devout, it was a destructive tool used by infidels to lure the followers of Islam into a life of sin. A few family members who traveled to America and Britain to attend universities returned devout fundamentalists.

Osama bin Laden was not the first member of the royal family to act out against the corruption and decadence of the House of Saud. Mahrous bin Laden, Osama bin Laden's brother, befriended a group of Muslim youths from Syria called the "Muslim Brotherhood." In Nov. 20, 1979, just one month after the invasion of Afghanistan, one thousand young men from this movement took over the Grand Mosque of the holy city of Mecca, the traditional pilgrimage site of the Muslim world. During this time, the bin Laden Construction Co. was working under government contract to build and make repairs to the holy site. Mahrous bin Laden and fellow members of the brotherhood masked their entry to the area by using trucks and construction equipment carrying building supplies to the site.

The government sent in the Saudi Arabian National Guard, its most qualified force, to root out the malcontents. The battle raged for two weeks until the last of the brotherhood attackers gave up. One hundred and twenty-seven National Guard men died. One hundred seventeen of the Muslim Brotherhood attackers lost their lives. When his brother walked free from jail, Osama learned he could be forgiven for any crime against the government or the Prophet Muhammad. This was not true, however, of the young men of the brotherhood. The remaining sixty-three who had been captured were beheaded for their act against the state.

After a personal pilgrimage to Mecca, Osama was a changed man. Previously, he had had a reputation for being a debonair high school student who had led a decadent lifestyle. After Hajj, he shed his freewheeling ways to become a person of ultraconservative values. In 1979, just a few days after the

Soviet invasion of Afghanistan, Osama slipped out of Saudi Arabia and crossed the border into Afghanistan as a Saudi jihad.

The United States was the most powerful nation in the world, but it still would have been difficult to position forces in Persian Gulf without help from a local Middle Eastern state. The decision to go to war against Iraq may not have been made solely by the United States. The governments of Saudi Arabia and the United States have a history of cooperation. The kingdom does not have an all-powerful military. Its squadrons of naval vessels do not ply the seas to demonstrate power. Instead, the Saudi government uses money to grease the palms of powerful groups or individuals.

Take the Reagan administration's need for funding when it decided to battle communism in Central America Nicaragua in 1982. Contra guerrillas were attempting to overthrow the leftist government of Nicaragua, so the administration went to Congress, specifically to the U.S. House of Representatives, expecting it to approve funding for the campaign. When the house voted against the funding, the Reagan administration turned to Saudi Arabia, which provided the money: $1 million a month for a total of $32 million. The Saudis did not ask for anything special, just shoulder-fired anti-aircraft Stinger missiles. The administration went to Congress again, and again Congress refused to fund the sale of the missiles, refusing to give heat-seeking missiles to a Middle Eastern country that could become hostile to the U.S. So Reagan declared the missiles "emergency measures" and secretly flew 400 of them to Saudi Arabia as payback for the $32 million the Saudis spent helping the U.S. defeat the Nicaraguan government. Just as the kingdom of Saudi Arabia was there for Reagan when money was needed for the contras, the Americans were there for the kingdom when Saddam Hussein stood on the doorstep of Saudi Arabia during the invasion of Kuwait.

Saddam's invasion of Kuwait gave the royal family quite a scare. At the end of the First Gulf War, the American and coalition forces stopped short of taking Baghdad. By the time coalition forces entered Kuwait City, the Iraqi army was in full retreat. Had they pressed home their attack, it is probable that Iraqi forces could never have stood its ground. One theory is that the coalition forces had expended their ammunition in the drive into Kuwait and may not have had enough bullets or bombs to carry the charge into Baghdad. The more logical reason, however, is weapons of mass destruction (WMD). The U.S. knew Saddam had chemical weapons because it had provided them. For Saddam to lose Kuwait would be a disappointment, but not an act that would unseat him from power. Had coalition forces stormed Baghdad, Saddam would have used every weapon at his disposal, including chemical weapons. This would have bogged down the attack, potentially turning the fight for the city into a bloodbath. Fighting in chemical-warfare suits is cumbersome, and a soldier's maneuverability is restricted. Tanks would have become easy targets in confined streets.

The U.S. provided chemical weapons to both sides in the Iran-Iraq War, wanting to see the Iranians defeated without missing an opportunity to sell them weapons. As the war progressed, the Iraqi Army did not prove its mettle. The Iranians launched wave after wave of infantry attacks at Iraqi positions, pushing them back inside Iraqi national territory. The American administration became uneasy. The oil fields of Saudi Arabia had to be protected at all costs. So the American government stepped up its support to Baghdad. Intelligence gathered by satellite was given to Iraqi forces to turn the tide of war. American advisers also began taking a larger role in training for attacks and coordinating them. All this showed early promise, but it still failed to give the Iraqis the advantage. Things began to look more desperate. The U.S. issued instructions to the Centers for Disease Control to begin providing biological material to Iraq. This material included viruses, retroviruses, bacteria, fungi and tissue with bubonic plague and West Nile virus.

The American government's fear of Iraqi weapons of mass destruction is not exactly a fabrication. The government and military needed to know for sure that all chemical agents had been disposed of before launching any attack. If they launched too early, securing the oil fields could have been extremely difficult because Saddam would have doused American troops with chemical agents.

No doubt the Iraqi people were thankful to escape the yoke of Saddam. He was a tyrant who killed thousands of his own people. He regularly watched and participated in torture for entertainment and raised two sons more sadistic than himself. In one famous televised session of government, he announced a list of alleged traitors who were then taken away to be executed. Those members of government who weren't on the list were to be the firing squad for the alleged conspirators. The American government wanted the Iraqi and the American people to see the invasion of Iraq as a war for freedom and a way to get rid of weapons of mass destruction. However, the Iraqi people and the majority of Americans had trouble believing the intent of the Bush administration.

As part of the deal to end the First Gulf War, the United Nations established a special commission (UNSCOM) to ensure the destruction of Iraq's long-range missiles and weapons of mass destruction. The United Nations Special Commission, led by Swedish diplomat Rolf Ekéus, conducted team inspections inside Iraq led by the venerable American Scott Ritter. (Ekéus later became Sweden's ambassador to the U.S.) From 1991 to 1998, UN inspectors spent countless hours combing through documents, searching buildings and military bases and interviewing individuals. Under Section C of Resolution 687, the job of the commission was to supervise the elimination of all missiles with a range of 150 kilometers (93 miles) or farther. Officials believed some of these missiles were destroyed in the war but that 200 had survived.

During Operation Desert Storm, United Nations forces expended a great amount of resources to stop the flight of SCUD missiles into Israel and Saudi Arabia. The missiles themselves were not particularly accurate, but if fitted to carry chemical agents and launched into a crowded population center, they would have had the potential to do great harm. During the war, Coalition military Special Forces and fighter aircraft patrolled Iraq, bombing targets thought to be missiles.

Medals were conferred and promotions given based on the number of missiles destroyed. Publicly, the military waged a very successful campaign to destroy these missiles and their launchers. However, it was not until after the war and by an investigation by UNSCOM that the government learned that not one SCUD missile was destroyed by the aircraft hunting them or by the Special Forces. Over the course of the inspection process, the UNSCOM team learned that the Iraqi government destroyed these missiles to comply with the treaty. However, the government did attempt to hide engineering drawings and molds from which new missiles could be manufactured. Even after proof of the missiles' destruction, the CIA continued to insist that 200 still existed.

Ensuring the cooperation of the UN resolution was not only important for the CIA but also for British Intelligence (MI6), Israeli Military Intelligence (IMI) and Iraqi intelligence (Mukhabarat). Sanctions were crippling the Iraqi economy and Saddam wanted them stopped. He gave the order for all stockpiled missiles and weapons of mass destruction to be eliminated. To comply with UNSCOM, the Mukhabarat sought special permission from Saddam to interview scientists and military officials to ensure the order was carried out.

The CIA initially had a major role in collecting information that could be passed to UNSCOM teams during their inspection. U2 flights were supposed to be made at the time weapons inspectors were on the ground to give up-to-the-minute information. Unfortunately, as time went on, the inspection team learned that information given to them was misleading: U2 flights scheduled to fly over Iraq were rescheduled, and they did not fly over their targets at agreed-upon times. Because of such information provided by the CIA, inspectors were sent into places that proved to be dead ends. Ritter and his inspection team then turned to MI6 and IMI for information.

For UNSCOM, working with Israel was a sensitive issue. The American government did not trust Israeli intelligence. If Arab governments had discovered Israeli involvement, they might have stopped supporting the inspections. While UNSCOM was still receptive to information from the CIA, its most accurate information came from MI6 and IMI.

The failure of the American administration's policy over Iraq was glaring. Popular support for Bush Jr. slipped to a low of about 30 percent (January 2007). The press and many Americans have been under the impression that the CIA was forced by the Bush administration to find evidence of weapons of mass destruction no matter what. However, the decision to attack Iraq was made in October 1991 during the presidency of George H.W. Bush. The CIA implemented a two-part policy called Containment and Containment Plus. Containment isolated Iraq from the rest of the world while Containment Plus focused on the elimination of Saddam. To manage this operation, the CIA formed an operational team within the Directorate of Operation called the "Iraq Operations Group." The group began by broadcasting messages over the radio in support of the Iraq National Congress (INC), an anti-Saddam organization led by Ahmed Chalabi. The goal was to build a force in northern Iraq that could secure the northern portion of the country from the Iraqi army; however, political divisions within the INC and the American buildup of forces in Kuwait persuaded the White House to drop the support for the INC in 1994.

This was replaced by a CIA lead *coup d'etat* launched under the auspices of United Nations Inspection Team 150. The plan, "Silver Bullet," would organize a group of Iraqis to topple Saddam from power. It appeared to the U.S. government that the economic sanctions placed on Saddam by the UN were failing. Placing sanctions had strengthened the power of Saddam and weakened the position of the United States. (Ultimately, these sanctions would hurt the American war once American and British forces conquered Iraq.) Prior to the invasion of Iraq, the Americans assumed that the Iraqi economic infrastructure—roads, ports, airport, communications, hospital and energy distribution— were modern and in good repair. This was either a fool's assumption or a lie intended to reassure those who were unsure about an invasion. Either way, when the Americans took Iraq, they found a country in ruin. Its economy and infrastructure needed billions of dollars in repairs.

The plan was for the coup to be executed in the third week of June 1996. Under the cover of inspection team UNSCOM 150, the CIA would place communication assets that would transmit signals to coup leaders to signal the uprising. However, on June 26, the CIA's Amman Station received a message from Iraqi Intelligence saying the CIA's coup was compromised. The CIA was depending on defectors who were actually Mukhabarat double agents. In fact, Tariq Aziz, Iraq's deputy prime minister, and the Mukhabarat had the most accurate view of the situation. They knew what the CIA was going to do and when. They knew all or most of the players involved and they knew the UNSCOM inspectors were not part of the plot. The CIA Amman Station quickly evacuated, and all traces of CIA involvement were erased.

Approximately 100,000 Iraqis were killed between 2003 and 2011 in the Iraq War and occupation. Sectarian violence at one point nearly plunged the nation into a civil war. Iraqis who suffered the most from the conflict were not combatants, but civilians kidnapped, raped and murdered in sectarian violence. Living conditions have not been positive since the invasion of American and British troops. One byproduct of U.S. involvement was that graft, always a part of the business environment in Iraq, ballooned to drastic proportions.

One figure surrounding this corruption was the leader of the INC, Ahmed Chalabi, described as a portly MIT graduate from a wealthy banking family. The information he passed to the CIA and U.S. Department of State before the war was, at best, unreliable. Nevertheless, the strategy to develop Iraq into a prosperous country by the Pentagon stemmed from Chalabi's leadership and recommendation.

After the invasion, the American administration assembled a group of inexperienced managers from the U.S., some recently out of college, to repair the nation's infrastructure and bring its government up to working order. James Dobbins, RAND analyst and reconstruction expert, described these young administrators as "heroic amateurs," passionate and conservative to be sure, but nevertheless doe-eyed and inexperienced.

The initial rebuilding estimate for Iraq sounded great to the government and to American families. Just one week after the attack on Iraq, Bush announced a rebuilding proposal of just $2.4 billion. This would go toward repairing the country's electrical and oil systems and toward funding humanitarian aid. From the beginning, this figured sounded low. However, Paul Wolfowitz, deputy secretary of defense, assured lawmakers that Iraq's $100 billion in oil reserves was capable of paying for itself.

One of the first contracts was awarded in secret to Kellogg, Brown and Root (KBR), announced by its former CEO, Vice President Dick Cheney. Halliburton was awarded $7 billion to put out oil-well fires in Iraq; a total of nine were extinguished. The next month, the government awarded San Francisco's Bechtel Corp. $680 million to rebuild the nation's infrastructure to include bridges, schools, hospitals, roads, and power and sewage plants. Unfortunately, economic sanctions had resulted in years of neglect to Iraq's infrastructure. The equipment used to run the oil and electrical systems were old and outdated. They were kept working by a patchwork of repairs done with whatever supplies were available. Essentially, the system was ready to be scrapped, not repaired.

In September 1993, the White House revised estimates for the reconstruction. Iraq would need $5.7 billion for the electrical system, $5.1 billion to rebuild the military, and $3.7 billion for water and $2.1 billion for the oil industry. Despite hesitation by Congress, the White House received nearly all the funding it requested. The president hailed the decision as the "greatest commitment of its kind since the Marshall Plan."

However, what ensued was corruption and incompetence on a massive scale. The list of failed construction projects is long and its accomplishments few. There was no communication system when former Army Gen. Jay Garner, director of reconstruction and humanitarian assistance of Iraq, arrived in Baghdad. Reconstruction officials were using satellite phones that often failed to connect with callers in the U.S. People just down the street from each other did not have phones or radios to communicate with each other. USAID proposed to build a cellular phone network in Baghdad. Problems with issuing the contract ensued when San Diego-based Qualcomm wanted to use its Code Division Multiple Access (CDMA) to best its European rival that was using Global System for Mobile Communications (GSM). A lobbyist for Qualcomm contacted Congressman Darrell Issa, R-Calif., arguing that an American company should receive the contract to rebuild the country. Congressman Issa sponsored Resolution 1441, which would have forced the government to give preference to American companies. The resolution also provided that any cellular contracts awarded would go to a company using CDMA technology. The bill failed to pass.

The first cellular phone contract was awarded in late May 2003 to MCI by the Defense Department. Later that summer, three more companies were to be chosen to purchase licenses to operate in Iraq. To position itself to win the contract, Qualcomm partnered with a consortium called Liberty Mobile, run by Irish Internet businessman Declan Galway. When the Department of Defense awarded the license, Liberty Mobile did not get the license it sought. Qualcomm then had a stroke of luck in Jack Shaw, deputy undersecretary for International Technology Security. Shaw was a former political appointee during the Ford, Reagan and Bush Sr. administrations. He abruptly lost his job when the Democrats took control of the White House. With the election of Bush Jr., he once again found employment with an appointment to the Defense Department. The title provided him with an office and staff in the Pentagon C-ring, but very little work until his old friend Don DeMarino introduced an associate with Liberty Mobile, Declan Galway.

Meanwhile, the reconstruction money pot for Iraq had grown large and deep. Sen. Ted Stevens from Alaska wanted a piece of it for his state. In the 1970s, Alaska Native Corporations' were established to settle outside territorial claims for native Alaskan tribes. The rights of these corporations allowed them to sell oil, mining and timber rights in order to provide impoverished tribe members with an income. In the 1980s, many of these corporations teetered on the verge of bankruptcy. In the 1990s, the Alaskan senator introduced a series of bills that would allow the federal government to award unlimited no-bid contracts to small businesses run by native corporations. This gave defense contractors a loophole to exploit. The native tribe could receive a no-bid contract from the government and contract the work out to large corporations like Bechtel or Halliburton.

One of these native corporations was NANA Pacific. Its specialty was sewer and water systems engineering, and corporate officials were after a contract to dredge the harbor of Umm Qasr. Officials at Liberty Mobile realized that by collaborating with NANA, they could get the cell phone contract without having to bid. At that point, Undersecretary Shaw decided Iraq needed a police radio system. This system would allow Iraqi police to communicate with Iraqi security forces. He contacted his new friend Declan Galway at Liberty Mobile and negotiated an alliance. NANA Pacific would get the cellular contract in the no-bid process and then subcontract the job to Declan under a new company, Guardian Net. First, the contract needed the approval of Iraq's Ministry of Communications and its senior adviser, Daniel Sudnick, a former military officer and communications engineer for AT&T. When the cellular phone contract was announced that summer, Qualcomm lost the bid and one of the other bidding companies filed a protest. Needing help, but unaware of the business alliance between Shaw and Qualcomm, Sudnick turned to Shaw for assistance. Shaw gave Sudnick the help he was looking for, Bonnie Carroll, widow of an Alaska National Guard general.

In Washington, the installation of an emergency communications network became the highest priority. Sudnick returned to the U.S. and briefed Paul Wolfowitz, Colin Powell, Dick Cheney and Condoleezza Rice about the communications system. Upon his return to Iraq, Sudnick got down to business. In March, he received a message from Shaw ordering him to contract the job to NANA Pacific using the CDMA technology and for Guardian Net to build the system. A couple days later, NANA Pacific sent a follow-up email to Sudnick, ordering him to allow the new police system to be configured with the ability to offer nationwide commercial cellular service. This piqued the curiosity of Sudnick and Carroll, who understood the police communications network to be for police only. As they dug through the paperwork submitted by Shaw and NANA Pacific, they learned Guardian Net and Liberty Mobile were the same company and that Shaw was the prime manipulator of the scheme. Upon the request of Sudnick and Carroll, the coalition canceled the NANA contract. Two days later, on March 9, a Sunni sheik named Sami Majoun walked into the communications office and asked Carroll to go for a drive. As it turned out, Sami was the newly appointed Iraqi minister of communications, appointed in secret by Shaw. Fearing for her life, Carroll turned down the ride. Later, in an interview with a *Mother Jones* magazine reporter, Sami was overheard by a translator admitting to fellow associates to being in business with Liberty Mobile. In Washington, Shaw was working overtime to ruin the career and reputation of Sudnick by spreading rumors of corruption. On March 23, Scott Redd, deputy of operations to Director of Reconstruction and Humanitarian Assistance Paul Bremer, summoned Sudnick into his office and fired him from his senior adviser position. In December 2011, Shaw was forced to resign.

After Sudnick's return to the U.S., he reported his concerns to the Pentagon Inspector General's Office. The case was referred to the FBI. Because of his continued actions, his superiors decided he was mentally unfit to carry out his job and he was fired from his job with the federal government. The police communications systems would take another two years to complete, a delay that may have caused the continued fatalities of American and Iraqi soldiers. On July 30, 2007, The FBI and IRS conducted a search warrant on Stevens' home in connection to his links to an oil-services company (VECO) and fisheries. However, after Stevens was convicted, the U.S. Department of Justice dropped the conviction, citing the prosecution's inability to follow proper legal procedure and an inappropriate relationship between a lead agent and a star witness. The department then opened an investigation into the members of the prosecution. In August 2010, when Stevens was on a fishing trip with four other people, his plane crashed into the side of an Alaskan mountain.

The invasion of Iraq by forces from the West was not completely without merit. From a military and strategic standpoint, it was the right thing to do. Iraq is the center of gravity in the Middle East. Nearly all forms of trade or communications travel through Iraq, and its geographical location makes it the center of Middle Eastern politics and ideas. It keeps the radical Iranian government from crossing swords with the House of Saud.

Chapter 12

Until 9/11, terrorism was something done in other countries. Terrorists were here in America, but they confined their activities mostly to money-raising. Organizations like the Irish Republican Army financed its war with England from citizens here in America. Middle Eastern groups like Hamas (Harakat al-Muqawama al-Islamiyya) and al-Qaeda had been in the U.S. raising money but had had little interest in conducting high-profile attacks back then. Prior to the first attack on the World Trade Center, such groups concentrated on fund-raising and public relations campaigns to raise awareness of their causes.

As the war in Soviet Afghanistan ended, returning jihad warriors were rejected by their home countries. Their governments did not welcome these trained killers, skilled only in the handling of weapons. Because many of these governments were already unpopular with their own people, they feared the returnees might take up arms against them. Lonely men without education or skills are potential time bombs, even for socially well-adjusted countries. Governments were willing to support them as long as they stayed in Afghanistan. But they returned to a society that rejected them. They had no jobs, no education and no women to marry. War and conflict were what they understood. Unwelcome in their countries, the returnees did the one thing that made the most sense to them. They returned to their old ways.

In time, many of the returnees reconnected with old comrades, and these comrades stayed in touch with their leader, Osama bin Laden. In 1990, many left their home countries with airline tickets paid for by bin Laden to Sudan. The Sudanese government opened their borders and hospitality to al-Qaeda. In its newly found country, al-Qaeda began to reconstitute into an international terrorist organization, complete with corporate offices. It established officers of logistics and added a CEO, CFO, public relations/marketing department, training and a mission statement. Al-Qaeda was already entrenched in

America. Beginning in 1970, its headquarters had been in New York and New Jersey. From the East Coast, cells branched west to California, Arizona, Florida and Michigan. They set about recruiting and raising money for jihad in Palestine and Afghanistan. With a border as long and porous as the United States, getting into the country was the least of their worries. Many applied for student visas, and, once inside the border and out of sight of customs officers, they simply disappeared, blending into the population.

Sept. 11 was not the first Muslim terrorist incident in New York, nor was it the first attack on the World Trade Center. Some early terrorist crimes went unnoticed by law enforcement and the federal government, which passed them off as common crimes. One of these was the assassination of a radical, outspoken rabbi known for his anti-Arabic rhetoric. Meir Kahane, 55, was outspoken in his attempt to expel Palestinians from Israel. His killer, El-Sayyid Nosair, 31, an Egyptian member of al-Qaeda, attended his meetings for a year before killing him. On the day of his final speech, Meir stood in front of the ballroom at the Manhattan Marriott Eastside Hotel. Nosair entered the ballroom with a coat draped over his arm, drew a .357 handgun from his waistband, walked to the front of the hall and stopped at the edge of the crowd. He smiled, dropped the coat and fired the handgun twice, hitting the rabbi in the neck and killing him. Nosair sprinted for the door, but was grabbed around the leg by Irving Franklin, 70. Nosair fired again, hitting Irving in the leg, and ran outside, intending to catch a pre-positioned cab, driven by co-conspirator Mahmud Abouhaima, another Egyptian. However, the cab had earlier been ushered away by hotel security. Nosair jumped into another cab, surprising driver Frank Garcia, who drove one block and stopped at a stoplight. Nosair jumped from the cab and ran down the street, waving his gun.

When U.S. Postal Inspector Carlos Acosta saw a man running at him, waving his gun, he drew his own sidearm and shot Nosair in the neck. Inside Nosair's wallet were newspaper clippings of important local events and three fake drivers' licenses and addresses. Arriving at the suspect's home six hours later, police found the co-conspirator taxi driver and another accomplice, Mohammed Salameh. In Nosair's home in Cliffside Park, N.J., police discovered bomb-making manuals, maps of New York landmarks and instructional manuals printed by the U.S. Army in Special Forces tactics. Also found was a list of important Jewish citizens and Israeli government leaders and a receipt for 1,440 rounds of 7.62mm ammunition used in the Soviet AK-47 assault rifle. Although police immediately suspected the plot to kill the rabbi was much bigger than just Nosair, New York City officials misevaluated the evidence and then lost it altogether.

The FBI was the second agency to arrive at the home. Officials took evidence to the local FBI office. Two days later, Manhattan District Attorney Robert Morgenthau claimed jurisdiction over the case and moved all evidence into police custody. From this stage, the New York City Police narrowed the investigation from a potential international terrorist incident down to a common crime. The evidence taken from the home remained in storage and unevaluated. Ignoring evidence to the contrary, police decided this was a lone gunman, a shooter with a grudge. In fact, Nosair was not the lone gunman. The FBI also believed him to be part of something much bigger, a possible link to a terrorist cell or cells, which they believed to be forming in the country. Instead, the case remained with the district attorney's office where the court acquitted Nosair of the murder charge, finding him guilty of only possession and assault. The court sentenced him to seven and half years, and his legal defense was paid for by a man later made famous for the attack on the World Trade Center, Osama bin Laden.

Even at the national level, terrorism seemed to be much more of a nuisance than a real problem. The first attack on the World Trade Center took place on Feb. 26, 1993. Al-Qaeda operatives drove a rented van into the underground parking garage and exploded it, causing enough damage to kill six people and wound 1,000 others. The intent was to bring both buildings down on top of one another; however, the bomber miscalculated the building's size, leaving it intact. Both the Americans and al-Qaeda came away from the incident having learned lessons. However, the American government was much slower to realize the extent of the terrorists' capabilities, a mistake to be repeated in Somalia.

The American government did have its successes. Because of the political pressure, the FBI and CIA worked together in full cooperation. Right away, the serial number of the vehicle used in the World Trade Center attack was tracked to a Ryder rental van company in New Jersey. The next day the renter of the truck, Salameh returned to the rental company to reclaim his deposit, saying the truck had been stolen. The clerk told him he needed a police report to receive his deposit. When he returned with the report a couple of days later, he was captured by the FBI.

After this, the cooperation between the two intelligence organizations broke down. Political infighting tore the fabric of trust needed to work together. Without America's intelligence agencies in top form, al-Qaeda was able to carry on its fight, eventually causing the worst terrorist attack on American soil.

It also proved that the enemy understood U.S. strengths and weaknesses much better than the Americans did.

Americans can be a giving people. They like to trust charities and their work. Giving to charities makes people feel that they can give with an open heart. The Holy Foundation was one of the largest fund-raising organizations of 2000, raising $13 million. So vast and complex was its operation that it took the FBI nine years to collect enough evidence to shut it down. This large, well-known and well-respected charity worked with some of the most respected American corporations. People could donate by shopping at Home Depot. They could go online and contribute through Amazon.com, and the receiving company would match the donation with a donation of its own. In return for their donations, donors might be sent photos of a child in Palestine, whom they thought were helping to save.

However, much of the money went to the families of suicide bombers and airline tickets for radical clerics coming to the United States to deliver fiery sermons. Corporations were not the only fund-raisers; individuals played important parts as well. Lebanese Shiite Mohamad Youssef Hammoud was just sixteen years old when he began training in a Hezbollah paramilitary camp. At eighteen, he came to the United States and took permanent residence in Charlotte, N.C., a popular Palestinian-American town. Here, he met and recruited other local Shiites through group gatherings. Friends sang Hezbollah songs and watched videos of attacks on Israel. They listened to taped messages of sermons given by radical Muslim leaders and became conditioned toward militancy. Once conditioned, they turned to fund raising, not a violent form of support, but probably the most crucial to carrying out the bombings and attacks against Americans.

The group of young fund-raisers heard about other Shiites from the area smuggling cigarettes from Charlotte to Detroit and making as much as seventy-five cents per pack. In North Carolina, the tax ran just five cents. The group began smuggling cigarettes. Each week they loaded 1,500 cartons of cigarettes inside a large van and drove north to Detroit, sometimes selling to Shiite gas stations along the way. In

Detroit, the cigarettes were sold to Shiite storeowners who sold them with the regular tax of seventy-five cents and pocketed the profit. Each trip produced a tidy sum of $10,000. Hammoud became quite successful. He opened a tobacco shop, which allowed him to buy at wholesale prices. Then he opened a restaurant to launder the money. The money made from smuggling cigarettes was in the millions of dollars, all of which was wired to Hezbollah.

On these road trips, the fund-raisers came in frequent contact with law enforcement officers who gave them tickets for speeding and parking violations. Within one year, the van was stopped five times, and police confiscated $62,000 and two million cigarettes. North Carolina law enforcement, the FBI, ATF and INS agencies began investigating the group's activities. After a four-year investigation, 250 law enforcement officials in Michigan and North Carolina arrested eighteen people on money laundering and racketeering charges.

In North Carolina, authorities discovered the group had also been involved in identity theft, Social Security number fraud, and production of fake credit cards and stockpiling of weapons. The investigation also uncovered some startling facts about the government's immigration policy. On June 6, 1992, Hammoud had entered the United States with three other relatives using an obviously fake passport. Instead of turning him back at the border (airport), he was allowed to enter pending an investigation. After five months, he filed for political asylum saying Israeli-Lebanese allies were out to get him. After thirteen months, his application went to court and he was ordered deported. Hammoud appealed the court's verdict. Case backlog delayed his hearing. One year later, in December, he married an American named Sabina Edwards and applied for permanent residency. After eighteen months, authorities discovered Sabina Edward's birth certificate was counterfeit and the marriage was false. Again the court ordered his deportation. Hammoud relocated and simply vanished from the system. In 1997, the records show a "marriage" to Jessica Wedel and, a few months later, to Angela Tsioumas, who was already married.

Hammoud eventually was granted an alien green card, even though INS had the records of the fake passport, multiple marriages and deportation orders. INS overlooked the first marriage to Sabina. They then overlooked the orders for deportation and the false marriages. Finally, in 2002, the court sentenced him to 155 years in prison for aiding a designated terrorist group.

America's open society has left us vulnerable. Problems arise with trust. We have no choice but to become more security conscious, even at the sacrifice of personal freedom. In the past, both the FBI and CIA have conducted surveillance operations against American citizens for purposes of politics and not of national security. What would happen if members of the government, their associates or agents were to use the FBI information collect about citizens for profit?

As with most information systems, the greatest threat to the DCS 3000 (Digital Collection Systems Network) would come from the inside. Since they have access to the system at various levels, users could damage, alter or erase and destroy system hardware and software. They could also use the information gathered by it for profit by passing on the collected information or by altering those being monitored.

History suggests that people, including government officials, business associates or agents themselves, attempt to collect such information for use outside "official business." The collective intelligence apparatus, in a sense, becomes an ally to the enemy, and the American intelligence system becomes a double agent unto itself. How do you give a lie detector test to an entire double-agent organization?

Chapter 13

One day I was born and people told me I was righteous. I got married and had a child; they were righteous too. My righteousness went to battle; God was on its side. Now, someone has taken my righteousness and I am just a man.

Anonymous

On Sept. 10, 2001, we were still a young country swaggering through world politics like a heavyweight boxer. On Sept. 12, we were scrambling to count our friends and enemies. The world had turned out to be a much more dangerous place than we thought.

On the morning of Sept. 11, President Bush was in an elementary school classroom in Sarasota, FL, reading aloud to a circle of children. By the time the second plane hit the second tower of the World Trade Center, all of America sat glued to their television screens. Inside the classroom, Capt. Deborah Loewer, director of the White House Situation Room, whispered to White House Chief of Staff Andrew Card, who confirmed to Bush that America was under attack. Press Secretary Ari Fleischer held up a sign in large lettering for only the president to see that read, "Don't say anything yet." Bush nodded and continued reading The *Pet Goat* to the children for eight to nine minutes before setting the book down.

What transpired next will forever be a matter of debate. In the small plush underground Situation Room in the White House, a discussion regarding the evacuation of family members of the Royal House of Saud was underway. A request was brought to Richard Clark, chief counter-terrorism adviser to the National Security Council, to let citizens of Saudi Arabia leave the country. The answer from the White House to Clark was yes. Clark said later, after he'd left the White House to run a consulting firm that he didn't know who sent the request, but it was either the FBI or the State Department, both of which deny giving approval.

Within hours of the destruction of the World Trade Center, American airspace was shut down. Aircraft could neither enter nor take off from within U.S. air space. As it turned out, no one (except Saudi Arabian nationals) was allowed to leave the U.S. According to a White House official, the evacuations never took place. The FBI refuses to confirm its part in the evacuation of members of the Saudi royal family. However, a prominent member of the House of Saud and close friend of Bush, Prince Bandar bin Sultan bin Abdul Aziz, identified as "Ambassador E. and P of the Kingdom of Saudi Arabia," confirmed live on CNN, the FBI's work in organizing the flight of Saudis out of the county. The FBI did indeed play a critical role in the organization and reparation of members of the House of Saud to leave the country on 9/11.

On Sept. 11, at 4:30 p.m. two private detectives, Dan Grossi and Manuel Perez, escorted three young Saudi men onto a private Learjet from Tampa, FL, to Lexington, KY. According to the *Tampa Tribune,* one of the men was a member of the royal family, the second was the son of an Army commander and the third was an unknown. In Lexington, the three boarded a larger aircraft with other members of the royal family, including a man named Prince Ahmad bin Salman, nephew of King Fahd. Prince Ahmad was known as a racehorse enthusiast, an owner of many fine horses: War Emblem, Sharp Cat, Lear Fan, Royal Anthem and Triple Crown Winner and Point Given.

On the morning of the attack, a sale of racehorses was underway in Lexington, KY. Upon news of the attack, officials postponed the sale until the following day. The next day, Prince Ahmed attended the sale and purchased two horses. In a statement to the media, Prince Ahmed remarked, "America is home to me. I am a businessman. I have nothing to do with the other stuff. I feel as badly as any American and extremely astonished. ... We have terrorism in Saudi Arabia and we know how painful it is."

Six months later, in the early morning hours of March 28, 2002, a plane touched down on the outskirts of Faisalabad, Pakistan. On a tip from the National Security Agency, American commandos and members of the FBI landed, deploying electronic jamming equipment to block local communication towers, including police and mobile phones. Commandos surrounded a two-story home owned by a banned militant Muslim group, lashkar-e-Toiba. A commando peering through the window blinds from the outside could see a fax machine light, a man sleeping on a cot and others sleeping on the floor. At 4 a.m., the commandos smashed in the door and raced into the house, moving quickly from room to room. The occupants inside grabbed for weapons. The man on the cot dashed for the back door and was shot and wounded. The operation took twenty minutes.

The FBI handcuffed thirty-five Pakistanis and twenty-seven men from other countries and loaded them into vehicles. During the operation, four suspects and two FBI agents were wounded. One of the suspects, a Syrian, later died. As suspects were loaded into a van, the FBI checked each face against a picture. None of the non-injured suspects matched the photo. They then checked the injured lying on stretchers against the photo. Bingo, a match! The man shot while trying to escape out the back door fit the photograph. His name was Zayn al-Abdin

Hohamed Husayn, a.k.a. Abu Zubaydah, a key member of Osama bin Laden's inner circle and a prime suspect. Abu Zubaydah was bin Laden's chief of operations, responsible for training between 10,000 and 100,000 recruits in eastern Afghanistan. He planned plots to blow up Los Angeles International Airport and the Radisson Hotel in Jordan. Zubaydah had served as field commander for the attack on the destroyer USS Cole in port at Yemen. He also briefed Richard Reid, the failed shoe bomber, prior to his flight from Paris to Miami. The NSA tracked Zubaydah by his phone number, which was found on the mobile phone of Djamel Beghal when he tried to blow up the American Embassy in Sarajevo, Bosnia-Herzegovina.

Once his medical condition was stabilized, agents began interrogations to establish Zubaydah's identity. Each time he denied it; however, agents did not need him to say yes. All they needed was a voice recording to match his voice with the voice in a phone conversation. The recording was a match! Over the next two days, doctors continued to monitor Zubaydah's medical condition, allowing agents to question him. To relieve the pain, doctors put him on a narcotic drip to make him comfortable. The narcotic allowed Zubaydah to remain lucid throughout the interrogation. If the FBI decided to turn the drip off at any time, the pain from the wound would be immediate. Doctors remained close by to monitor his condition so that he would not slip into a coma from slowed breathing or psychosis. For forty-eight hours, interrogators conditioned him for questioning by keeping him awake by alternately turning on and turning off the narcotic drip. At first Zubaydah was tepid about answering questions. Once he knew his identity was confirmed, he became more cooperative.

Zubaydah was taken to an American Special Forces base in Kandahar, Afghanistan, and placed in a room built to resemble the inside of a Saudi jail. His interrogators placed him on a thin mattress with steel springs to keep him less than comfortable. The machines by his bed resembled medical equipment used to monitor patient's vital signs. Instead, they measured voice and heart rhythms for truthfulness. Here, he was questioned using the good guy-bad guy technique. At first, agents expected him to cooperate with the U.S. and fear the Saudi authorities, who wanted him for questioning. They figured he would understand that the Americans would do what was necessary to keep him alive as long as he remained with them. Once he was in the hands of the Saudis, Zubaydah probably knew would never leave prison alive.

FBI agents began by asking three questions for which they already had the answers. After half an hour of questioning, Zubaydah was placed on a drip of thiopental sodium, truth serum. Under light, this drug makes a person lose their inhibitions, which can be fought if they know they are on the drug. In this case, he could not have known because all the drips looked similar, and some were to alleviate pain. During questioning Zubaydah was hard to crack.

When the Americans questioned him, he refused to answer. They got nothing. When Saudi agents entered the room and took over the questioning, Zubaydah began talking freely. He went from being uncooperative to animated, eager to speak.

Unbeknownst to the Americans, he'd been working closely with the Saudis. It was the Americans he feared. At this point, he requested that a phone call be made to a senior member of the Saudi royal family. He was able, from memory, to provide names and phone numbers of key royal family members. One of those was Prince Ahmad bin Salman bin Abdul-Aziz, nephew of Fahd and chairman of the Saudi Research and Marketing Group.

The Saudi agents left the room but returned hours later. They told Zubaydah he was lying. They said the prince denied everything, and the phone numbers he provided were wrong. Zubaydah became even more determined to provide information about Saudi and Pakistan leaders. He said he had been present in 1996 when bin Laden met and made a deal with Pakistani Air Force Cmdr. Mushaf Ali Mir. In that meeting, the commander promised to supply protection, arms and supplies to al-Qaeda. Zubaydah also detailed a meeting with bin Laden, in which bin Laden talked about speaking with Saudi Intelligence Chief Prince Turki in Afghanistan. Prince Turki and bin Laden had brokered a deal. As long as bin Laden kept the war away from Saudi Arabia, the government would provide aid and not seek bin Laden's extradition. The Saudis sent money on a regular basis.

Zubaydah dealt personally with several members of the royal family through intermediaries such as Prince Sultan bin Faisal bin Turki al-Saud, former military pilot and nephew of Fahd, and Prince Saud bin Turki bin Saud al-Kabir. In fact, both Prince Ahmed (flown out of Lexington, KY, in an FBI-coordinated flight) and Mir were briefed before the Sept. 11 attacks. Neither knew specific details, but they knew an attack would be made on that date. Later, when Zubaydah learned the Saudi agents were FBI agents, he denied everything and attempted to hang himself, using a bed sheet.

The American government went to the governments of Saudi Arabia and Pakistan demanding explanations. Both gave the same answer, that the claims were false and malicious and that, had they known, they would have passed on the information. On July 22, 2002, the Saudi government announced the death of Prince Ahmed. The cause of death was a heart attack. The next day the government announced that Prince Sultan bin Faisal bin Turki al-Saud, 41, had died in an auto accident on his way home from a cousin's funeral. The following week they made a third announcement. Prince Saud bin Saud al-Kabir, 25, was found dead. He died of thirst while traveling in the height of the summer heat. Seven months later, the government of Pakistan announced the death of Musahf Ali Mir and his five children. Their plane crashed in the unruly Northwest Frontier Province. Their Fokker airplane had passed a recent fitness and maintenance inspection.

Chapter 14

Since the beginning, Americans have looked to the East Coast for its direction in policy and money. I think, in the future, America's West Coast will have more wealth then the East Coast, which leads to power and political clout. The West Coast has the resources; it has the intellect, land and technological innovation to place people into space, which could create jobs and wealth and a trade route. Trade routes, when dominated by a company or a country, generate significant wealth. If America were like a European country, then the wealth would be generated by and for the country as a whole. Since it is not, California will probably dominate the space economy, leaving the other states and the federal government very uncomfortable with the swing in power.

Much attention has been placed on terrorist attacks made on the East Coast. However, the struggle to protect home ground is taking place all across the nation, including California and the San Francisco Bay Area. In fact, one of the country's first al-Qaeda terrorists, Ali Mohamed, was discovered in Santa Clara, Calif., just a one-hour drive south of San Francisco. Mohamed had begun his career in the Egyptian Army where he trained in intelligence. He quit after shifting political alliances within the Army put his career in jeopardy. He went to work as a counter-terrorism expert for Egypt Air, then went to the CIA and asked to work as an informant to the CIA. The CIA terminated the relationship after Mohamed spoke openly of his employment to friends who had possible terrorism links. The American government then placed his name on a customs watch list, should he try to enter the country. One year later, he did just that. He applied for and was granted a visa to visit the U.S. Once in the U.S., he joined the U.S. Army and received orders to work as a supply sergeant for a Special Forces unit at Fort Bragg. He excelled as a soldier, giving classes about jihad, terrorism and Middle Eastern affairs at the John F. Kennedy Special Warfare Center and School. During his enlistment, and against orders from his superiors, he took a leave of absence to fight in Afghanistan during the Afghan War. He returned to the U.S., proudly displaying belts worn by two Soviet soldiers he allegedly killed in battle. While in the Army, he visited New York, where he taught terrorist tactics to jihadists living in New York. One of these people was El-Sayyid Nosair, who served time for assassinating a rabbi in New York. When Nosair was investigated and his house was searched, Army Special Forces manuals belonging to Mohamed were found.

After his enlistment ended in 1989, Mohamed moved to Santa Clara to live with his wife, whom he'd met on a plane returning from a trip to Europe. In Santa Clara, he worked as a security guard and owned a home computer business. Between 1989 and 1998, his terrorism activities surged. In the early 1980s, he joined the Egyptian Islamic Jihad and made frequent trips to the Middle East to train terrorists in the art of surveillance at bases in Sudan and Afghanistan. He traveled to Africa and scouted the American embassies in Kenya and Tanzania. His work would later lead to the bombing of both embassies on Aug. 7, 1998.

At some point, Mohamed had worked for both the CIA and the FBI, though neither was aware of his employment with the other. During his employment with the U.S. government, he was heavily involved in terrorism. He openly bragged to fellow terrorists about his employment with al-Qaeda and the American government. While living in Santa Clara, he was sent by the FBI to infiltrate local mosques. Once inside, he told the members he was working for the FBI. It is feared that instead of spying on the terrorists, he gave away U.S. secrets to them.

While working for both U.S. Army and intelligence agencies, he seriously undermined the security of the nation. He seemed always to be a couple steps ahead of the American intelligence agents who were supposed to be controlling him. Finally, in September 1998, Mohamed was arrested in Sacramento as he prepared for a flight to the Middle East. He was indicted in May 1999 and has since disappeared from public view. In the history of double agents, he may have been one of the most damaging to the U.S. All indications point to his being a part of the planning in the bombing of the World Trade Center. Mohamed had intelligence training, which allowed him to properly judge the building's strengths and weaknesses. This information was, no doubt, passed on and used in planning the attacks.

On the morning of Sept.11, 2001, televised pictures of the planes smashing into the World Trade Center were seared into my mind as I commuted to my job in downtown San Francisco. The city was a ghost town. Most companies had completely shut down. However, the owner of the company I worked for at that time was a former Vietnam infantry officer. He was not one to give into terrorism, and consequently the office remained open. That afternoon I left work and walked to the Bay Area Rapid Transit (BART) station on Market Street. The corner of Sutter and Market was deserted, except for an Arabian man on the opposite corner. Another Arabian man rode briskly past me on a bicycle and halted abruptly in front of the man on the corner. He jumped from his bike, and the two men embraced in what appeared to be a celebratory embrace.

This seemed odd and it left me feeling uncertain. I wondered if I should go to the police. I decided against it.

The next year was tumultuous for San Francisco. Thousands of demonstrators—old hippies and new—from across the nation and other countries took to the streets to protest the invasion of Iraq. In San Francisco, the downtown financial district was racked by two weeks of protest. Crowds, both large and small, moved from street to street staging sit-ins. Individual protesters chained themselves together in defiance over the government's policy to invade Iraq. In some cases, the police had to separate people with bolt cutters. In other cases, protesters locked arms inside metal sleeves. Famed '60s folk singer Joan Baez led a sing-in at San Francisco City Hall, to a rendition of "Let's Break Bread Together." During the day, helicopters hovered over the city, relaying crowd information to the police below. The protesters attempted to shut down the Bay Bridge and financial district. The police arrested thousands of demonstrators, some who protested in peace. Others arrived at events armed with slingshots, firing bolts and knives to slash police-car tires.

Using computers and cell phones, protesters coordinated their movements in a "sit-and-disperse" tactic. Individuals would suddenly gather at a defined location and stage a sit-in, blocking traffic. As the police redeployed to the location, the group would disband and scatter, only to reappear in another location. The protests drew people from all walks of life, such as Lea, 34, who told reporters, "My brother is on his way to Kuwait. He's in the Army. He doesn't support the war. No one on our family supports this war." Another group of observers, Brad and his family, watched from Chinatown. "This is a great education for the kids," said Brad. "It's like watching the news as it happens. There's nothing like this in Phoenix."

The police did their best to provide for public safety. Businesspeople were warned that Molotov cocktails had been placed in bushes along the popular protest route of Eleventh and Howard streets. One of these locations was in front of the Four Seasons Hotel. However, no bottles were found. Officers suspected protesters ditched the bottles before officers could catch them.

The first couple of days of protest were the largest. Parents who had protested in the '60s brought their children to take part. The San Francisco protest spawned protests in other large cities and small towns across the country and around the world. The next week there were more protests, but these were small and went mostly unnoticed. It's possible that terrorists may have helped plan the Bay Area protests. San Jose was the headquarters of Ali Mohamed and may continue to be an area of interest to people with terrorist ties seeking to operate in the San Francisco Bay Area. Information released by the FBI in 2004 "included evidence that al Qaeda operatives surveyed the Bank of America tower in San Francisco and considered it a 'location of interest,' " as well as East Coast financial institutions, according to the *San Francisco Chronicle*. Although information about surveillance of the 52-story landmark at 555 California St. was limited, the San Francisco

FBI assured residents that the threat was taken seriously and extra security measures were taken.

Israel has had a tough time catching bus bombers before they strike, and the U.S. government feared that this tactic would be imported and used against the American population. On a weekday morning during commuting hours in 1993, a nervous Middle Eastern man stepped onto a San Francisco Transit (MUNI) Bus carrying two pieces of luggage. The first was a school backpack filled with clothing, the zipper near bursting. The second was a large, hard-shelled suitcase. A lock from a doorknob had been installed on the side of the case. The young man appeared nervous. He never let go of the hard-shelled suitcase and exited the bus at the Greyhound bus station. Two weeks later, the FBI announced that "al-Qaeda and other terrorist groups are likely to single out commercial transportation like planes, trains and buses. ..."

Sept. 11 was a tragedy, a life-altering event for those inside and outside the area surrounding the World Trade Center and the Pentagon. The fear born of that day will be forever seared into the bodies and the minds of those touched. The aftereffect was great and is permanent. The explosion tore America's sense of being and of safety. It threw the government into survival mode. Those in power who created and enacted policy and laws to ensure stability were heavily scrutinized and appeared shaken as a result. But out of the ashes appeared a new American, one dedicated to freedom and tolerance and democracy. This new person is strong and wise, faithful to its God and a cause of justice. This new American committed wrong, was wronged and can forgive: Our country survived.

Chapter 15

Moses went up from the steppes of Moab to Mount Nebo, to the summit of Pisgah, opposite Jericoh, and the Lord showed him the whole land. ... And the Lord said to him, "This is the land of which I swore to Abraham, Isaac, and Jacob. I will assign it to your offspring. I have let you see it with your own eyes, but you shall not cross there.

Deuteronomy 34.10

Theology, history and the present day oftentimes intercede. As people, we like to think we have grown, we have learned, and thus it is unlikely that we will repeat the past. However, this is usually not the case. Technology may have changed us, but human behavior has remained consistent since the dawn of biblical time. The writers of the Bible and Torah and Koran wrote history as best as they could because the stories changed as they were told from person to person. It is possible, even with technology like Google and Wikipedia that the way an event happened will continue to change in the telling. People still hear what they want to hear. Thus history often repeats itself.

The U.S. of today, for instance, could learn from studying the time surrounding the French Revolution. A brief history of 1776 through 1802 shows these to be nervous years for France. Prior to 1776, France was at the peak of its power, controlling a large part of world trade and setting the cultural pace for the civilized world. In these countries, most people spoke French in addition to their native tongue; if one did not speak French, one was not considered educated. Because France was considered the most civilized country of its time, peoples sought to emulate all things French. King Louis XVI's opulent palace in Versailles was not only the place for the social elite, but also the home design to copy.

However, for those at the bottom of society—the third estate— life was tough and getting tougher. French economy and personal wealth were derived predominantly by agriculture. France was a major player in world trade but did not produce enough food to feed its citizens. Those who owned land were much better off than those who rented land or those who owned no land at all. When planting seasons were good, there were enough jobs and the economy thrived. If crops failed, however, the poor went hungry or starved.

French citizens of the middle class, considered part of the third estate, owned land, homes and generally served in the armed forces. In the army, officers could purchase the rank they wished to hold. If one wanted to ascend the ranks of the army, they paid in cash. In the navy, rank was attained with hard work, dedication and merit. However, the army usually proved more successful in battle. Life for the upper class—the second estate—was relatively easy. This population, though less than 2 percent of the population, held about 20 percent of the land and paid virtually no taxes. Those who had money and wanted a government or high church position or an army commission could purchase one. They could also win court judgments or prevent judgments from being passed against them by having the case transferred between court jurisdictions, keeping the case in legal limbo. Young men could ascend the ranks of bureaucracy without the inconvenience of putting in years of dedication and hard work.

Citizens of both the second and third estates could join the first estate, the clergy, which made up about 5 percent of the population and held about 15 percent of the land. The clergy provided many public services: schools, records, relief to the poor. The lower clergy came from the third estate and resented the higher clergy, who came from noble families. Most of the government's revenue came from taxing citizens of the third estate: taxes paid for traveling from town to town, taxes paid to the owner of the land they farmed, taxes paid for foods. Then, of course, there was the tithe paid to the Catholic Church. When the crop season was good, half the money earned by these citizens went to purchase food to feed their families. When the crops failed, the poor spent three-quarters of their income on food. The Church paid no taxes, and the nobility paid few taxes and received nearly all the coveted career occupations. As time went on, however, the price for admission into career positions increased, putting a greater financial strain on the second estate.

Prior to the years 1776 to 1802, France enjoyed good-to-moderate crop yields that successfully fed the population. However, the country's population outgrew the country's ability to feed it. Once the food supply decreased and prices increased, members of the third estate were denied health, prosperity and homes. They stopped paying their mortgages and many went from homeowner to homeless.

Poverty was everywhere, resulting in large bands of vagabonds who lived in the forest and countryside and preyed on at farmers and villages. During times of moderate prosperity, this population numbered about 8 million. When the good times ceased, this terrorizing population could rise by a further 3 million. Institutions providing food and services to the poor increasingly couldn't keep up with the need. Monasteries had to cut back the amount of food they could feed to the poor. Increasing numbers of women turned to prostitution to feed themselves and the children they raised. The country's economics and its system of laws allowed the rich to get richer while the poor remained poor or slid further into poverty.

The American Revolution of 1776 had a profound effect on the history of France, England and America. If France had not come to the aid of the beleaguered American colonial army, America's capitol city could still be London. This is not a sure bet, however, since many British colonies eventually became self-governing. France's involvement in the American Revolution was a boon for America, which eventually won independence, but it wiped out the national budget of France. Its bankruptcy, in turn, led to the collapse of the government and was a precursor to the French Revolution.

Ego was behind the decision of the French government, under King Louis XVI, to side with the Americans and their war for independence. France had lost vast resources on the American continent when it lost the Seven Years War (1754-1763). And joining the conflict gave the French government a grand opportunity to get back at the government of Great Britain. The controller-general (treasurer) warned Louis that the country's involvement in America's fight for independence would push the country into insolvency. This warning proved unpopular and he was replaced, but his replacement financed the war by taking out loans from the Church, organizations and other countries.

The more France became involved in the American conflict, the more precarious its finances became. Raising taxes was never popular, but the government obscured the war expenses by listing it as "extraordinary accounts" on treasury financial statements. Thus the amount of true debt was not discovered until the king was faced with debts the nation could not afford to pay.

The next government treasurer understood that taxes had to be raised to pay the debt, but Parliament refused. The war cost France 1,066 million *livres*, which escalated after the American Revolution was over due to the high interest rates France was charged for its loans. In 1786, one quarter of the state's income was in deficit; nearly half of the annual revenue collected went toward the loans; more than half of the following year's revenue was already spent to pay down debts.

France's economy was already bad in 1788 when a freak July hailstorm brought further devastation. Hailstones large enough to kill man and beast destroyed hundreds of miles of crops. Even in normal times, surviving the winter months was difficult, but the subsequent summer disasters shattered the economy, and food prices finally peaked a year later, in July 1789.

People were mad and hungry. They wanted a return to stability, and they wanted someone to blame. They knew the government, the pillar of French society, was not helping the situation, but the people focused their attention on secretive groups like the Freemasons. The people believed such groups manipulated members of government, and thus the nation's economy. The people also blamed securities speculation (stock market short-selling) and government conspiracies. All of this fueled their angst. They were also affected by the success of the American Revolution. To them, the American farmer was an icon of freedom. If the Americans could do it, then so could the French. *Viva la Révolution!*

The French Revolution was not a single revolution. Instead, it was a series of many smaller civil wars pitting the government against the people, villager against villager, and group against group. The French people entered the period of 1776-1802 with great enthusiasm. Theirs was a collective feeling of *ancien régime,* which meant leaving behind an old set of laws and societal mores that no longer worked. Replacing them would prove to be much harder than they thought, however, for many policy changes made in the throes of revolution were reversed after the revolution to, once again, benefit members of the second estate—the nobility.

Attacks by neighboring countries ended the French Revolution. Despite internal strife, the people of France were victorious, at first, in beating back invading armies. Enter Napoleone di Buonaparte, then a little-known Corsican artillery officer. He seized control of France by way of *coup d'état* and reversed the decline of the nation's psyche by going to war with other states. Napoleon would become one of history's greatest generals until his defeat at Waterloo and his exile to the island of Saint Helena, where he officially died of "stomach cancer," which, arguably may have been arsenic poisoning.

Historians love to study the French Revolution because of the profound effect it had on the rest of the world. They either love or hate Napoleon. Yes, he enacted social and legal changes that brought France back to prosperity. But he also had turned cannons filled with grapeshot onto French protesters in Paris. The "whiff of grapeshot," as the action was later called, ended a national insurgency and secured Napoleon as the leader of France.

The French system of education and finance needed immediate repair. Only the rich or very gifted had access to education, and since the Catholic Church did the educating, religion came first, with reading, writing and arithmetic a distant second. While this benefited clergy and law students, it ignored those in the middle class who administered the military and public works. To solve this crisis of education, Napoleon established *école centrales*, a system that taught middle-class children to become military and public works professionals. Training and pay for teachers was improved, and educational standards were standardized across the country. Students who showed a talent for learning were admitted with scholarships to *lycées*, upper-level secondary schools that prepared students for university studies.

Napoleon also left a legacy of laws still used today. The Napoleonic Code officially separated church and state, giving French citizens religious freedom and reigning in the privileges of the clergy. The feudal order, which had dominated French society, also became illegal. Individuals now had the right to choose their own professions, whereas before, one's profession was handed down at birth and determined one's lifelong social standing. In marriage, women also gained some property rights and the right to divorce their husbands. Later, women would lose more legal rights then they held before the revolution.

Since the main cause of the revolution was government debt, tax codes were revised and a government tax collect agency formed. Prior to this, individuals purchased the position of tax collector, which gave them a right to collect taxes in their respective area. Taxes were increased in some areas of the country, and the government bought bread to distribute to the poor. A national bank was established, which, over time, brought needed stability to the financial system. However, many of the economic policies that were passed after the revolution were later gradually reversed to favor the rich once again. Money was also coined, which gave people greater confidence in the national currency. Finally, a national public works projects was instituted to build canals, roads, schools, seaports, national monuments and a fire brigade for Paris. Napoleon brought significant changes to France, which made him very popular with the French people and prepared the nation to succeed in a new and changing world.

The people of France and the United States have more in common then they realize. Oftentimes, the two governments bicker. Oftentimes, the French and American people compare themselves with one another, sometimes approving, sometimes not. But sometimes people argue with those they care about the most. They look into the mirror at the other and recognize traits they dislike in themselves. And so, looking at America in the new millennium, the years 2000-2012 appear to be "nervous years," perhaps a mirror image of France in the years 1776 to 1802. Like France in pre-1776 years, America was at the peak of its power pre-2001, controlling a large part of the world trade and setting the cultural standard. America has risen to technological prominence and wealth as yet unsurpassed by any other country. America—a society of dreamers and risk-takers—took the innovations of historical greats and molded them together. Even 230 years after its founding, the citizenry still champion the goals of presidents Washington, Franklin and Lincoln. Despite their own state of moral imperfection, Americans strive for perfection and demand moral perfection of the world.

Much of the American experience today mirrors the French experience during its revolution. The American government went to war with Iraq out of spite, not ego. Like the French involvement in the American Revolution, war nearly bankrupted both countries.

Like France, America's banking and housing sectors collapsed. Like the people of France. Americans turned their interest to secret societies such as the Freemasons. Though they didn't turn to prostitution like the French, great numbers of American's married women who could not find jobs elsewhere turned to work in the phone sex industry. People formerly with middle-class incomes, homes and solid work experience survived any way they could, living with relatives and in cars and parks.

Like France, America needs to rebuild its country's infrastructure—roads, dams, bridges. Unlike France, it has opted instead to invest in more military technology. Like France of the 1700s, the American tax system is in shambles, and schools need updating. The rich in America are getting richer and the poor are getting poorer. Only 40 percent of Americans pay taxes, and many corporations are exempt from paying any taxes at all. The government, at times, fails to provide what is needed in national emergencies. For instance, the Bush administration showed impaired judgment and limited management in responding to the needs of the people of New Orleans in 2005 when Hurricane Katrina hit the city. For days people were trapped without food and water in a flooded area with death and disease all around them. And the city has still not fully recovered.

The destruction of the port of New Orleans crippled the national economy, which then went into further decline when a housing bubble imploded. The collapse of the housing bubble was followed by a collapse in the banking/investment system, and the country slid closer to economic ruin. Prior to the collapse, American investors had become enamored with hedge funds, unregulated high-risk investments. These funds were originally available only to the wealthy who could afford to risk hundreds of thousands of dollars. However, pension managers jumped on the bandwagon, investing workers' retirement funds into these high-risk investments. These workers could ill-afford the huge losses and will receive far less in retirement then they expected. Even without searching, America has found its *ancien régime*—a system of finance, education, business management and health care that can neither support nor be supported by a middle-class American family.

The U.S. rose to unmatched prosperity in the twentieth century, but now—100 years later—the rules for economy and governance have changed. The old way of doing business will lead to no business at all. America can no longer be the world's consumer. Its homes are over-priced, health-care costs out of control, and the nation's education system is in decline. Americans are house-poor, cash-poor, under-educated and falling into ill health, all factors that decrease the country's competition with the European Union, Japan and the emerging countries of China, India and Brazil.

History will mark the 9/11 attack as an enormous event in American culture. Ultimately, Americans may decide the Iraq War was necessary and its outcome favorable to democracy, but its management was characterized by mismanagement.

Lack of planning by the White House, lack of understanding by the Pentagon and mismanagement of the reconstruction showed an American government ill-prepared to occupy Iraq. In time, the battle for Iraq was won, but the victory was not born of great leadership. The war in Iraq was won by the privates, sergeants, lieutenants and captains going out each day to kick in doors, collect information and chase bad people down dark alleys. The soldiers' bravery and expertise allowed Washington, over an extended period, to begin to understand the complexity of the situation in the Middle East and Iraq and finally form a winning strategy. But the human and economic costs were devastating to the Americans and the Iraqis.

The presidency of George Bush, though not perfect, did have one success: It did not allow another terrorist attack on American soil. This important issue has been overshadowed by other issues. Without the work of the CIA and other government agencies, even more devastating attacks could have taken place. Pressure techniques placed upon captured enemy combatants, as imperfect as they are, were necessary to keep the country safe. The CIA should not be forced to apologize for applying such techniques to those people who would, without remorse, have done much worse onto us. However, the CIA's failure to uncover the 9/11 plot prior to its inception is inexcusable.

But when the 2008 election rolled around, Americans wanted change. They threw away the old system and took on decidedly more risk by voting the lesser-known Barack Obama into the White House instead of frontrunner Hillary Clinton. Voting an African-American into office was a chance to help heal the voices of the Civil War and to establish a national personality. Prior to the election, America's personality was a borrowed personality from old Europe. Its voice, goals and vision of itself stemmed from ideas long ago. They were the values of transplanted European Americans who sailed into Jamestown, Va., in 1607.

Many fear America is a nation in decline, that it is a has-been, a nation put in its place by its politics. Looking back, we can opine that policing the world is not as grand as imagined. The economic and political cost to the country is tremendous, and eventually what goes up must come down. America is a nation of risk-takers, not inclined to move at a measured pace. Space exploration is our future, and the West Coast will take the lead. Those who can control trade routes in space will succeed beyond other nations. The cost will be high in people and investment; some will make great fortunes and others will lose them. This will be possible, not because of the old régime, but because of the new social changes taking place inside the country. For this great nation to move forward, it must be smarter, faster and healthier. This means improved health care, education and retirement systems to prepare the nation's citizens for what is to come. The nation will do all this, and it will succeed. Our forefathers, God bless them, would be proud!

Eventually all things merge into one, and a river runs through it. The world was cut by the world's great flood and runs over rocks from the basement of time. On some of the rocks are timeless raindrops. Under the rocks are the words. And some of the words are theirs. I am haunted by waters.

A River Runs Through it and Other Stories, Norman Maclean

Selected bibliography

The following includes some, but not all, of the periodicals and websites used as background for this book.

Ahmed, Nafeez Mosaddeq. *Behind the War on Terror: Western Secret Strategy and the*
 Struggle for Iraq. Gabriola Island, Canada: New Society Publishers, 2003.

Aita, Judy, "Ali Mohamed: The Defendant Who Did Not Go To Trial,"
U.S. Department of State, May 14, 2001. Downloaded from http://www.usinfo.state.gov archives.

Associated Press, "Documents show FBI spied on King's widow," Aug. 31, 2007.
    http://www.usatoday.com/news/nation/2007-08-31-king-fbi_N.htm

Benjamin, Daniel. *The Age of Sacred Terror.* New York: Random House, 2002.

Bodansky, Yossef. *Bin Laden: The Man Who Declared War on America.* Rocklin:
Prima Publishing, 1999.

"The Clergy and the Nobility/The French Revolution," Big Site of History: History of
Civilization,
http://bigsiteofhistory.com/the-clergy-and-the-nobility-the-french-revolution.

Brown, John. *The United States Army in Somalia, 1992-1994.*
CMPH Publishing 70-81-1,

United States Army. Last updated Feb. 24, 2006,
http://www.history.army.mil/brochures/Somalia/Somalia.htm.

Bulwa, Demian. *"San Francisco: Bank of America Tower was
Considered as Potential Target,"* San Francisco Chronicle,
Tuesday, August 3, 2004,
http://sfgate.com

Calabresi, Massimo, and Timothy J. Burger, "Who Lost the
WMD?" *Time Magazine World,*
June 29, 2003,
http://www.time.com/time/magazine/article/0,9171,461781,00.
html#ixzz1spNVlKS0.

Dawood, N. J., trans. *The Koran.* London: Penguin, 1997.

Doyle, William. *The Oxford History of the French Revolution.*
Oxford, England:
Claredon Press, 1989.

JPS Hebrew-English Tanakh. Philadelphia: The Jewish

Publication Society, 2000.

Dunbar, John, "FBI surveillance: It's come a long way,"
Associated Press, Aug. 30, 2007,
www.usatoday.com/news.

Englund, Steven. *Napoleon: A Political Life.* New York:
Scribner, 2004.
Fattahi, Kambiz, "US Army Enlists Anthropologists," BBC
Persian Service, Washington.
    Last updated, Oct. 16, 2007. (Accessed Oct. 27, 2007.)
http://news.bbc.co.uk.

Finley, M.I. *The Greek Historians.* London: Chatto & Windus
Ltd., 1959.

Fitzpatrick, Sheila. *The Russian Revolution*. New York: Oxford University Press, 1994.

Hampson, Norman. *The French Revolution.* New York: Charles Scribner's Sons, 1975.

Hofer, Peter Charles. *The Brave New World*. New York: Houghton Mifflin, 2000.

Howard, Michael. *The Causes of War*. Cambridge, Ma.: Harvard University Press, 1983.

KTVU.com, "SF Police Find Cache of Molotov Cocktails," March 21, 2003.
(Accessed Sept. 30, 2006). http://www.ktvu.com.

Lichtblau, Eric, "Threats and Responses: Domestic Security; Warning of
    Possible Attacks on Big-City Buses and Trains," *New York Times,* April 3, 2004,
http://nytimes.com.

Lippman, Thomas. *Inside The Mirage*. Boulder: Westwood Press, 2004.

Maclean, Norman. *A River Runs Through It and Other Stories.* Chicago: University of
    Chicago Press, 1976.

McFadden, Robert D., and Joseph B. Treaster, and Maurice Carroll. *No Hiding Place:*
The New York Times Inside Report on the Hostage Crisis. New York:
Times Books, 1981.

Markham, J. David. *Napoleon for Dummies.* Indianapolis: Wiley Publishing, 2005.

Miller, Christian T. *Blood Money.* New York: Little Brown and Co., 2006.

Miller, John, and Aaron Kenedi. *Inside Islam.* New York: Marlowe and Co., 2002.

Perkins, John. *Confessions of an Economic Hit Man.* London: Plume, 2004.

Posner, Gerald. *Why America Slept.* New York: Random House, 2003.

Ritter, Scott. *Iraq Confidential.* New York: Nation Books, 2005.

Saikal, Amin. *The Rise and Fall of the Shah.* Princeton: Princeton University
Press, 1980.

Sire, H.J.A. *The Knights of Malta.* London: Yale University Press, 1996.

Solé, Jacques. *Questions of the French Revolution: A Historical Overview.* New York: Random House, 1989.

Symon, Fiona, "Clashes Expose Palestinian Divisions," BBC News Online, July 24, 2001.

Treece, Henry. *The Crusades.* New York: Random House, 1963.

Turner, Channing, "Feds Drop Case against Former Alaska Sen. Ted Stevens," Aug. 11,
    2011, Main Justice: Politics, Policy and the Law,
http://www.mainjustice.com.

Unger, Craig. *House of Bush, House of Saud: The Secret Relationship between the World's Two
 Most Powerful Dynasties.* New York: Scribner, 2004.

Williams, Lance, and Erin McCormick, "Al Qaeda terrorist worked with FBI: Ex-Silicon
Valley resident plotted embassy attacks," *San Francisco Chronicle,* Nov. 4, 2001, http://sfgate.com

Wood, David Bowne, and Bob Mahoney, *A Sense of Values: American Marine in an
Uncertain World.* Kansas City: Andrews and McMeel, 1994.

Yardley, William, and Liz Robbins, "Former Senator Ted Stevens Killed in Plane Crash,"
New York Times, Aug. 10, 2010, http://www.nytimes.com

Zelnick, Robert, "Aftermath," *Hoover Digest 2003, No. 3, War with Iraq,* April 30, 2003,
http://www.hoover.org/publications/hoover-digest/article/6996